Life Success

*A Practical Guide for
Making Your Dreams Reality*

David Michael Ferruolo

Elements of Life Success:
A Practical Guide for
Making Your Dreams Reality

Mountain Lake Publishing
PO Box 6421
Laconia, NH 03246
(603) 556-4360 voice
(603) 556-4361 fax
www.MountainLakePublishing.com

Editor: Charlotte Cox

Editorial Assistance: Janette Tomes

Insights & Inspiration: Jennifer P. Crews

Cover Design: Jonathon Gullery

ISBN: 0-9776412-2-8

Elements of Life Success. Copyright © 2006 by David M. Ferruolo. All rights reserved. No part of this book may be used or reproduced in any manner without written permission except in the case of brief quotations embodied in articles or reviews. For information write Mountain Lake Publishing, PO Box 6421 Laconia, NH 03246

Produced Exclusively in the United States of America

www.DaveFerruolo.com

Explore your potential to live the
Amazing adventure life is meant to be.

Contents

Introduction   v

Chapter One
Life is Calling   3

Chapter Two
What Are Your Dreams   13

Chapter Three
What Makes You Happy   25

Chapter Four
What Are You Made Of   39

Chapter Five
Putting it all Together   49

Chapter Six
Thought; The hidden Power   61

David Michael Ferruolo

Chapter Seven *Scripting Your Life*	71
Chapter Eight *Deciding to Fly*	81
Chapter Nine *The Importance of Goals*	91
Chapter Ten *Set your Goals*	101
Chapter Eleven *Goals are Alive*	133
Chapter Twelve *Take Action*	141
Chapter Thirteen *Confronting Fears*	155
Chapter Fourteen *Overcoming Obstacles*	175
Chapter Fifteen *Feel Your Way Through*	193
Chapter Sixteen *Affirmations*	207
Chapter Seventeen *The Difference Between Thinking and Knowing*	221

Chapter Eighteen
Support   231

Chapter Nineteen
Invincible Determination   243

Chapter Twenty
You Can Make It Happen   253

Acknowledgments   258

About the Author   261

Suggestions for Further Reading   262

David Michael Ferruolo

-Introduction-

A Call to Action

You have taken your first step towards creating the amazing adventure that your life is meant to be. On the following pages are the guidelines and processes to help you break old routines and negative thinking patterns which enslave you to a mundane and unfulfilled lifestyle. This book is a call to action; it will beckon you to look deep inside yourself and to discover your talents and your capacities. Change is not easy, and success comes through a determination to change your life for the better. This path is not always easy, but the reward of living your dreams is well worth your time and effort.

Effort in equals effort out, so work hard and follow through with each step. Have patience and allow what you put into motion to gain momentum and propel you forward toward what you desire. Do not give up; do not quit. Take one step and one day at a time. Live in the moment, and do everything you can do this day to build the stairway to tomorrow's successes.

Everything you ever needed to accomplish, all that you want in your life is within you right now. With the guidance given in this book, you can learn to tap into your hidden inner power and create an action plan that maps out the road to your dreams. Read each chapter slowly and take your time doing the exercises. Put thought and effort into the process. Get to know yourself and what makes you tick. This is a very important step towards a balance between harmony and success. Who says you cannot be happy and peaceful and successful at the same time? Anyone can make money, but success should mean that you are also happy.

Success does not mean you are a super millionaire. Or course, this might be nice, but being successful in life has little to do with money and everything to do with how you choose to live each day. The adventure of life is just that—an adventure. Every day, you should be content with what you have and where you are, but your should also strive to be a better person and achieve a better place. Success is living your life to the fullest and following your dreams.

So without compromise, delve into this book and make a commitment to find a better way to live your life. Change is available to you right here, right now! All you have to do is decide you want it. I know you can do it. I know you will succeed. If you want it bad enough, nothing will stop you. As you step into unfamiliar territory, congratulate yourself and be at peace with the knowledge that you are now succeeding. You cannot be the true success that you want to be if you are not happy inside.

As you work through this book and put your success plan into action, remember your primary everyday goals should be inner peace, harmony and happiness. With this in mind, every situation you encounter, positive or seemingly negative, will not affect your day adversely. You can go home every day with a smile on your face because you have total control of goal number one—peacefulness.

So go forth and change your life. I wish you all the blessings in the world and pray for your timely success. Your future is bright and unwritten. Take control of your life—it is yours to do with as you will. There is no better time than now. You have taken the first step towards improving your life. Now follow through by putting one foot in front of the other and going forward. Take one step at a time, one day at a time, and soon you'll be on top of the world!

Blessings,
Dave Ferruolo

"We were born to succeed, not to fail."
-Henry David Thoreau

David Michael Ferruolo

-Chapter 1-

Life is Calling

I didn't think I could handle it anymore. My back was seized with pain, and my body shivered uncontrollably. It was about three o'clock on a chilly California morning, and I found myself naked, dripping wet and nearly crippled with pain. Could I go on? Would I be able to?

The first nineteen years of my life flashed before my eyes, and it all seemed to come down to this one single night and the choice I had to make. It was much more than just a choice. It would turn out to be a defining decision in my life—a decision that would dictate the rest of my existence—my successes, my failures, and ultimately what and who I would eventually become.

It was the first morning of Hell Week, the most grueling week of training to be a Navy SEAL—the military's elite Sea, Air and Land guerrilla warfare teams. Over one hundred men started this Hell Week with Basic Underwater Demolition and SEAL Training Class Number 141 and, by the end of it, less than thirty would finish. Getting to the first day of Hell Week had been tough enough—seven non-stop days of no sleep and strenuous exercise had already passed. None of us, however, had a clue about what lay in store for us over the next week. During the day we were brought nearly to heat exhaustion, and every night we were kept nearly hypothermic. And through it all, we were wet and sandy from head to toe.

It began early Monday morning with an exercise, or evolution, they called the "steel pier." The SEAL trainers carried a brass ship's bell everywhere we went. Trainees were quitting–dropping like flies as, one by one, they either walked, ran or crawled up to the quitting bell that signaled their defeat. The only way to get out of training was to stand in front of the entire class and ring the bell three times. Many made that trip this Monday night. Some were crying, some were screaming, but all were at the end of their mental ropes. The choice was clear to all of us—suck it up or quit.

The steel pier evolution went on for hours. We had to lay naked on a cold steel pier while the instructors hosed us down with water and made us do sit-ups, crunches, leg levers and various types of push-ups. Every 30 minutes or so, we were told to jump off the pier into the Coronado Bay and tread water for a half hour or more. This was actually refreshing because the 62-degree water was much more tolerable than the brisk 50-degree air and the bone-chilling wet steel pier. Also, in the water, we avoided getting hosed down with even colder water!

Earlier that night, I had thrown my back out while landing a small rubber boat onto the rocks in high surf. It was midnight, pitch black, and there was no moon. In the pounding of the southern California surf, we had to land our small, five-man, inflatable boat, or IBS (Inflatable Boat Small, in military lingo) on a rock jetty in front of the Hotel del Coronado. As I jumped out of the boat to secure it to the rocks, a huge wave took the IBS and pitched it on top of me, pinning me beneath the formidable water. My teammates pulled me out just as I ran out of breath, and we made our way to the beach. The result was a pulled back muscle.

Lying on the steel pier had aggravated my back problem to the point of agonizing pain. I could barely move. I crawled over the pier and surrendered, letting my body roll off and fall into the chilly water. Treading water was now nearly impossible, and it was only with my friends' help that I kept my head above water. A few hours later, with no end in sight, I was not sure that I could manage this ordeal any longer. This was it. My dream of being a Navy SEAL was fading quickly, virtually over. I was physically exhausted, injured, and mentally demoralized — how could I go on?

With help from my good friends, Jim and Pete, I managed to make my way up to one of the instructors. "You quitting, Ferruolo?" he asked. I replied, "My back hurts. I can't tread water." "You quitting, Ferruolo?" he asked again. I stood there in shock. What am I going to do? I thought. I can't quit, but I'm not sure I have what it takes to continue. "Don't do it, Dave!" Jim yelled from the pier. He paid for that outburst with a hose jammed into his mouth for a few moments.

A medic came over to examine me, and for about 10-15 minutes, he helped me stretch out. It had little to no effect. I could barely stand erect, and pain radiated continuously through my body. The instructor said, "This is

Elements of Life Success

why we train so hard. In combat, we do not have the option to quit. If we get hurt, we continue or get captured or die. Do you want to ring out and quit, Ferruolo?" I managed a weak "No." "Then get back in the water," he commanded. "You're not a quitter. I can tell. You can do this. It's all in your mind. You're going to take this moment with you for the rest of your life. So what are you going to do?"

I felt my heart pounding. I visualized myself at graduation accepting my diploma from BUD/s (Basic Underwater Demolition/SEAL school).

I saw myself standing proud as a member of a SEAL team and wearing the revered Trident, the symbol of a Navy SEAL. I can do this, I said to myself. This is it, I realized, the defining moment of my life. Do I continue realizing my dreams or just walk away? My thoughts were pure and strong, and I was determined to complete this training.

"Thank you, Instructor. I think I'll go back and join my class now." He smiled and said, "Good for you, Dave." I turned and with the loudest voice I could muster I yelled, "HOO-YAH!" and ran back to the pier. My classmates were back in the water, still treading. I looked up and saw the sun peeking over the horizon. I could feel the warmth of the day coming. "Permission to rejoin my class," I requested from another instructor. He smiled for only a second and said, "Good to have you back. Now get your lazy ass in the water and finish this evolution!" I happily jumped in. I knew at that point without a shadow of a doubt that I would be a Navy SEAL. I had made my choice. My decision was firm, and I held thoughts of my success in the forefront of my mind every moment of every day from then on!

David Michael Ferruolo

Creating your life is a matter of choice—a choice to get into the game of life and put forth the effort to make your dreams come true. Achievement itself is a lifestyle, not an endgame. Being successful is not a destination at which you arrive; it is a decision about the way you live your life. Adopting a mindset of success and achievement, coupled with an optimistic, positive attitude, and the unwavering determination to make things happen will propel you toward the amazing adventure your life is meant to be. It all starts with a choice, so make the decision to take command of your life. A proactive lifestyle is not always the easiest road, but it is well worth the bumps and potholes you'll find.

If we can open our minds and fully believe in the unlimited possibilities of what life has to offer, we can empower ourselves to move beyond our limits and make our dreams come true. We are all born with the same tools; it is how we choose to use them that defines us. It is not circumstance or luck that separates successful from unsuccessful individuals, but the ability to make decisions and execute them that makes one's life fulfilling. In the words of the great lawyer, William Jennings Bryan, "*Destiny is not a matter of chance, it is a matter of choice; it is not a thing to be waited for, it is a thing to be achieved.*"

Everything that was ever accomplished or made by mankind started with a thought. Thoughts are the seeds of creation, sprouting from deep within our minds and blossoming into our outer reality through our will. Whether our intention is to create, to explore, or to accomplish, these ideas come into being through action. The most powerful thing to bring dreams to fruition is action. Once our dreams have been defined and we know what really makes us happy, we can begin to script our lives and make an action plan to propel our desires forward. There is an incredible power that comes from making *any* decision to move forward toward our dreams and desires.

Think of your own dreams and life goals, and imagine what actions it will take to bring them to fruition. Such a process, which enables you to rise to new levels of awareness about who you are and what you can accomplish, is extremely empowering, and this will give you the inner strength to carry through. By defining your dreams, you will find out who you are and what you want to accomplish. This is a powerful process that creates motivation and gives you the strength to move forward.

Take a look around at all the miraculous things this world has to offer you. Towering mountains, lush forests, and pristine oceans beckon with beauty and adventure. Cities, states and countries bustle with variety and multiplicity. An infinite plethora of cars, electronics, houses, clothes, watercraft, furnishings and jewelry surround us. There are millions of people to befriend and countless romantic possibilities at our fingertips daily. If the experiences available are limitless, then what do you want to do, what do you want to have, and where do you want to go? With all the unlimited possibilities in the world, and with the infinite resources available within ourselves, I believe anyone with the right attitude and motivation can create the life they want and deserve.

And yes, I do mean *deserve*. Know that it is not a matter of fate or luck that propels you toward achievement, but rather choice and determination. When you choose to venture out of your comfort zone, facing any fears of the unknown to follow your dreams, you deserve all the good that comes your way. Know that *you* can make it happen. Armed with positive thoughts and intentions, confidently go forth into the unknown and don't bother to look back. The world beckons. So stand firm in your power and know that amazing things are out there for the taking. All you have to do is choose what you want!

-Exercise 1-

The Pen Pal

Our world is such an incredible place, filled with amazement and wonder. Now imagine that you have a pen-pal from another world, another planet we just made contact with. This new friend wants to come and visit. Write your new acquaintance a letter in the space provided below and describe all the things this planet has to offer. Money is no object, so outline the places that you will take your pen-pal and all the adventures that will be available. Describe all the things you will see, learn and experience together. Be as detailed and thorough as you can.

Dear Friend,

Elements of Life Success

David Michael Ferruolo

-Chapter 2-

What Are Your Dreams and Desires?

What do you desire most? Fame? Health? Peace? Romance? What are the things you would like to change about your life? Is there somewhere you would like to visit or move to? Are you happy with your job, your home and your car? What things do you wish you could buy? Do you want to spend more time with your family? Are you happy with your level of health or fitness?

It is important to have dreams and aspirations. The trick is not to get too deeply attached to those desires. If you can create your want list without any expectations of what may happen – except that you will be happy and try your best to accomplish them – you will not be depressed or upset if some of them do not happen. You will be content to know that you tried your best and be able to move on to other items on your list. Contrarily, if you become consumed with the attainment of certain things, you may become disheartened and angry if they do not manifest themselves.

It is also very important not to focus negatively on what is lacking in your life. Focusing on what you do not have will only keep you locked in that place of lack and desperation. The spiritual law of attraction states that what you fix your thoughts on will inevitably manifest itself in your life. If your mindset is negative and pessimistic, you will find more of that attitude with every turn you take. If you are always focused on what you do not have, you will, according to the law of attraction, be surrounded by that lack always. Having an optimistic attitude and focusing on what you want in a positive way will inherently bring what you desire closer to you.

Even clinical psychologists agree with this concept of focusing on what you want rather than on the lack of it. Although most of them do not subscribe to the spiritual law of attraction, they do agree we will subconsciously create life situations that fulfill our deepest beliefs and expectations. If we believe deeply that we are not good enough and will never be able to achieve what we desire, we will unconsciously make decisions and take actions that are congruent with those beliefs. This thinking will ultimately keep us in that place of lack and discord.

Yet it is possible to break through these negative thought patterns and focus on what you do want and desire. Even if it seems unattainable now, thinking positively about your desire will bring the essence of it closer to you.

I always wanted to be an adventurer, visiting exotic destinations and hiking, trekking, scuba-diving and experiencing whatever the world has to offer. Africa, Tibet, Chile, New Zealand, Fiji, Australia all fired my imagination, but for years I made excuses about why I could not travel to these amazing places. Whether it was budget, business commitments, family obligations or the fact that I could not find anyone to go with me, I always had an excuse not to go. I thought you had to be rich or just very lucky to travel to these kinds of places.

Instead I would satisfy my need for adventure by hiking in local and regional mountain ranges. I would scuba-dive the local lake and nearby coastline. I would ski the mountains close to my house. And yet, I would dream about what it would be like to trek Kilimanjaro, ski the Swiss Alps, dive the Solomon Islands or ride horseback across Morocco.

Occasionally I would travel to my friend Scott's home in Colorado, and we would go hiking, rafting and skiing. I would routinely visit my mother in Florida and scuba-dive in the Keys. All of these trips had a common theme, however. They were all within my comfort zone. Every trip was always to a place I knew, or with a group of people I knew. I never ventured past the limits of my safety zone to any of the places I truly desired to go.

Excuses were easy. But the bottom line was that I feared going outside my security zone. My yearnings for exotic travel appealed to me on the surface, but at a deeper level my thoughts were negative. I had a pessimistic mindset associated with adventure travel. The fact is, I did have the time and could afford at least some of these trips, but I kept thinking I could not go—until one day when everything changed.

I had lunch with my friend Carol on a sunny fall afternoon. We had not talked in depth for several years. At lunch, she told me how she had spent the past three years hiking through Europe. I was blown away. Carol had been on three trekking trips! This was *my* dream! We spent the rest of lunch that day talking about where she went and how she felt about going alone with unfamiliar people. Somehow, talking to Carol about this type of trip changed my mind about it. Suddenly it all seemed so easy to achieve. What had been holding me back? I wondered. Fear? Insecurity? I couldn't name it. I do know, however, that talking to my friend helped shift my mindset from pessimism to possibility!

Carol was such an inspiration that I actually started to research different adventure trips. To my surprise, I found that my dream trips were not much more expensive than a vacation to Florida or Colorado. The biggest difference was the flight time! So I searched, and I found an affordable dream trip to Chile to trek in Patagonia. It was so easy. Within a few days, I had figured out all the logistics, and in a few months I would be living my dream.

When I started to focus positively on what I wanted and the necessary steps to make it happen, the trip fell into place very easily. I now expanded my search to another destination. I have always wanted to hike the Inca Trail and see Machu Picchu in Peru. I started planning and have now created a financial plan for the trip. I have also made a list of other places in the world that I would like to see over the next seven years.

David Michael Ferruolo

I did not know how I would be able to afford to go on one great adventure trip each year, but I just told myself it would happen. I routinely would set aside time to think about it, visualize myself there and tell my friends I would be going very soon. My positive focus paid off. My friend Carol introduced me to travel agent Kim at Penny Pitou Travel. I soon met Penny herself, and we worked out a plan for me to lead some of these trips. My dream was coming true. Now it was possible that not only would I go on at least one trip a year, but I would get paid to do it!

One should have many dreams—the more dreams, the better. A creative mind is a healthy mind. I don't mean that you should lose yourself in an illusionary, fantasy world, which is unhealthy. But maintaining a vision of your wants, dreams and desires in a realistic perspective keeps them alive. It also gives you some hope that there is a better way to live—a better life that is within your grasp. Knowing what you want and where you want to go tomorrow is very grounding, and it fosters a healthy attitude for living where you are today.

I find that many people, when asked, know exactly what they want, whether it is a new car, a different home, changing jobs, a new romantic partner or all of the above. But *why* they want these things and what changes will have be made if they attain their wishes are harder questions for them to answer. When you think about what you desire, you should also consider what changes will emerge in your life. I believe that peace and happiness are the most sought-after "wants" in today's society. These simple desires manifest in our minds as cars, homes, romances and gadgets, but sometimes when we look deeper into why we want these things, we uncover the core motives behind them. (I call these "motivational factors" and will discuss them in depth later in this chapter.) There are many motivational factors, but peace and happiness are always at the root of each one.

I have talked with hundreds of people, and I have asked them all the same question, "What do you want?" All the answers are very different, but very quick. People always seem to know what they want. But when I ask them "why" they want those certain things, the answers come slower and harder. So people know what they want, but they do not know why they want it. And with a little time and a bit of probing, the answer to why they want something is always the same! For the hundreds and thousands of different wants and desires are all prompted by one simple reason—happiness.

An acquaintance of mine deeply desires a sailboat. He doesn't just want an ordinary sailboat but talks of owning a 70-foot schooner. He dreams of sailing the Caribbean and letting the ocean winds be his guide. As long as I have known him, he has always wanted to move somewhere or do something extraordinary with his life. He has lots of stuff—a Corvette, a nice truck, a 40-foot fishing yacht and tons of other toys: motorcycles, snowmobiles, dirt bikes, even an airplane. Interestingly, none of these things really make him happy. He continually disparages all that he has, where he lives, his business, the local economy, his sub-contractors and even what he looks like.

When I ask why he doesn't just go and do the things he dreams of, the answers are always negative: I have to work. I hate to fly. I can never find anyone to go with me. It will be a waste of time. I have too many responsibilities. It costs too much. So he stays at home, literally, and never ventures out into the world.

The fact is, he owns a great business and makes very good money. He works mostly alone, and he does not have employees to support. He does not have a business location to maintain, and he lives at home with his parents. He is not married, has no children, and his dog stays at home with his mother most of the time, so leaving poses no problems at all. He has virtually no responsibilities whatsoever, except to himself. He has the means, the method and the opportunity to do whatever he wants, but he elects to stay at home and spin pipe-dreams of sailing the Caribbean on a 70-foot schooner. So he works long hours and acquires more money and more stuff, all of which just fills up his garage but can never fulfill his soul.

If we look deeper into this kind of desire, we may see that the essence of my friend's dream is freedom and autonomy—that would make him very happy. But he is not willing to use the freedom and autonomy he already has. Have you ever been in that situation? It is very important to find the motives behind your desires. Doing so will reveal the core of your being, what you truly stand for and how you want to live.

To find out *what* we truly want and need in our lives, we must first discover *how* we want to live. Knowing how you want to live will in turn reveal one of the most critical pieces of information you need – what steps you would have to take to fulfill your dreams and desires. How do you know how you want to live? This knowledge is sometimes elusive and most often remains hidden until you begin to mine nuggets of it from those moments when you are most happy.

To find out how we want to live, we must determine what our underlying motivational factors are. In those moments when we are utterly happy – when we feel totally and completely alive and when our eyes are wide open to the world – we will find what drives us. We will touch the essence of our core, the basis of our character, and we will know what we need to do to fulfill our lives completely.

-Exercise 2-

Listing Your Dreams

Make a list of your dreams and desires. Be detailed and be creative. Do not spend a lot of time thinking it over. Just take your pen and write. Put down as many as you can. Have fun with this exercise. Dream big, dream small—but just dream. You can always cross things out later. Cars, homes, a new relationship, money for schooling, traveling, clothes, a new career, a promotion, meeting your favorite star. Whatever you want, give it a name and write it down. So now relax, lean back, and start dreaming!

My Dreams and Desires:

_____

_____

_____

_____

_____

_____

David Michael Ferruolo

Elements of Life Success

David Michael Ferruolo

-Chapter 3-

What Makes You Happy?

What puts a smile on your face? In those quiet moments when you are living in total bliss, what are you doing, who are you with, and what are your surroundings? What are the circumstances that make you truly happy?

Many people focus on the lack they find in their life and think money, things or relationships will solve all their problems. Consider this: having countless toys, friends, or dollars are not necessary for your contentment. Yes, they may help ease the pain temporarily, but inevitably they will create just as many new problems as they eliminated. Nothing external can ever replace the dissonance in your soul. Contentment comes from within. Know that *you* are the cause of your joy or sorrow, and there is no amount of money, things or people that can change this fact.

All of these things, I believe, can actually make finding true inner peace harder. With money comes the easy ability to externalize searching for what makes you happy. When you have the monetary means, you can try to buy your way to happiness. This can, of course, make matters worse. True success, in my book, means being happy and fulfilled while living a good life. Being wealthy would be a great bonus, but it can never, never buy a blissful life! I learned this in a surprising way, a number of years ago.

A man walked into my scuba shop early one spring. He was very interested in taking diving lessons from me. We chatted for a while about the joys and adventures of scuba diving. I told him about the places I had dived and mentioned the local wrecks in Lake Winnipesaukee. He finally said he wanted to sign up, but he needed to know how much it would cost. I showed him the upcoming schedule and told him the cost was $395 for the class and about $250 for the snorkeling gear.

"Well, I'll have to think about that, Dave," he said. I was okay with the response, since only about one in ten people I speak with actually joins the class. A week or so later, he came back into the store with a $50 deposit. He asked me if he could pay the remainder over the next few months. I thought about it for a moment ... there was something about this guy that I really liked. He was always in a great mood and carried a big smile on his face. I remembered seeing him driving his car around town and smiling from ear to ear. "Sure," I said. "No problem." We negotiated some simple pay-off terms and drafted a contract. He was now in class and had all his gear—on account. And true to his promise, he paid his account off on time, smiling.

For every class, he would show up in the best mood despite the 45-minute drive from his work. He was a joy to have in class, and the other students liked him. He finished his class, and I didn't see him again until the following summer. He explained that money was tight—he and his wife were busy raising their children—and diving had to take a back seat for a while. I said I understood, and he looked at some papers I had on my desk and asked what I was doing. I told him I was running some numbers and trying to create a business plan for an adventure scuba travel service.

I told him how frustrated I was with my business and my life, and I was looking for an avenue to make some good money and get out of my current situation. His response baffled me. I was not expecting such wisdom from someone who was flat broke all the time. With a big smile, he told me that money would never make me happy, and that I was the only one who could choose happiness.

He must have seen the perplexed look on my face, because he laughed. "Dave, I used to bring in a six-figure income, and I was miserable. My family made me happy, but I never saw my wife and kids. All I did was work. I had all the cool stuff—new cars, nice house, big TV and entertainment center. We gave it all up to live here in New Hampshire and be happy. I have never been so fulfilled as to be able to be home with my family every night and weekend," he said. I was speechless.

He knew what made him happy—his family. He took a big chance and changed his life. He is broke all the time, but in terms of inner happiness, he is one of the wealthiest men I ever met.

So in those rare moments of contentment in your life, think about who you are and how you are, not what you have. If driving through the country with the warm spring breeze blowing through the windows gives you pleasure, then what does it matter if your car is a Toyota or Mercedes? Do not get fixated on money to solve your problems. This will only bring more stress into your life. Know that the true source of happiness is you and that nothing external can do the job for you. You may attempt to take refuge in the illusion that money will set you free, but know that it is you who chooses freedom not your bank account. Think about it: If money is the source of bliss, why are so many millionaires unhappy? Money does not create happiness. You may change your circumstances, but if you cannot change yourself, nothing will really change! The experience of being *you* will not change!

If you are frustrated and unhappy where you are in life right now, more money will still leave you unhappy. If you are a negative, pessimistic person with a propensity to complain, money will not change your outlook on life. The simplest way to change your life is to change yourself. Success and greatness grow out of character, not wealth!

Thinking of all the great things you can do with money is fine, but I want you to think of what makes you truly happy. In the past and currently, what are the things you have done, places you have visited, activities you engaged in that bring you joy? If you could create the life you want and deserve, would it not consist of all these things you find enjoyment in? So, it's really quite simple. Living a happy life is doing the things that make you happy.

How often do you allow yourself to do these things? Could you allow yourself to do these things more often?

Could you create a schedule for yourself to do these things more easily? It is so much more important to know how you want to live than what you want to do for a living or what you want to possess in your life. A life of simplicity lived humbly with love and gratitude is sometimes the most rewarding path we could choose. This is true "life success."

So I ask you once more: What makes you happy and what makes you feel alive? In which moments of your life have you felt the most powerful and centered with yourself and your surroundings? Take a moment and think of these precious times of fulfillment. Hidden within these moments are your core motivational factors – what drives you. Your motivational factors are the core driving values and beliefs that shape your visions about the world. I have identified ten basic core motivational factors. They are:

Achievement (attainment, accomplishment, completion, success, triumph, victory)

Authority (ascendancy, influence, power, superiority)

Control (dominion, organization, preparation, structure)

Exploration (adventure, enthusiasm, curiosity)

Excitement (exhilaration, elation, thrill)

Freedom (autonomy, free will, independence, self-sufficiency, sovereignty)

Health (conditioning, fitness, well being)

Strength (vigor, robustness, fortitude, potency)

Endurance (stamina, patience, resilience, determination)

Intimacy (closeness, connection, familiarity, love, friendship, understanding)

Passion (dedication, eagerness, devotion, fervor, zeal)

Safety (fortification, protection, refuge)

Security (shelter, stability, certainty, trust)

After numerous conversations with many kinds of people, I have found that most of us share several of these positive core values, but only one or two are dominant. To know truly what will make you happy and to discover how you want to live, you need to identify which of these core motivational factors are your driving forces. For it is these core factors that are the inner triggers to your fulfillment.

When we are not aware of our motivational factors, we choose materialistic wants that result in actions of instant gratification or fulfillment. If we can understand directly why it is that we desire something, we can consciously and intelligently choose what we want, and reflect on whether those wants are in our best and deepest interests or if they are simply vehicles for instant gratification. When our core motivational factors remain unknown to us, we can create destructive patterns and bad habits in our lives. On the other hand, identifying our dominant motivational factors will allow us to move away from these negative tendencies and begin to positively script our lives the way we want. Knowing that a sailboat is just a metaphor for freedom will help you see which path you need to forge so that freedom will be more abundant in your life.

Sometimes our routines and habits can be clues to what our motivational factors are, and give us the reasons for how they can influence our destructive tendencies. Without our awareness, our subconscious mind will lead us into circumstances that it believes can bring satisfaction to us, based only on the need to fulfill a void in our lives and souls. If our lives are fulfilled with the self-knowledge of what motivates us and where we truly want to be in life, there will be no voids to fill. We can then consciously, intelligently, make decisions that are more congruent with our life path and not be so reactionary in our routines. This awareness breaks the bonds of old habits, which are based solely on instant gratification and need fulfillment.

It is important to identify our unhealthy habits and unconscious routines, so that we can stop reacting simply to unfulfilled needs and instead take conscious steps towards security and happiness.

There is a man who likes to go the bar several nights a week. He drinks too much and routinely hits on many women. He is known as a barfly, a drunk, and is very annoying to the single (and the not-so-single) women he encounters. He says he loves to party, but he always seems sad when he leaves at the end of the night. Where do you believe this man's destructive habits stem from? What are his motivational factors for being at a bar night after night? Could it be the motivational factor, Intimacy, that drives him? Perhaps it is this missing Intimacy, as well as the need for Excitement, that sends him seeking out strangers in bars?

A woman stares out the window of her office, frustrated with the day's workload. She pictures the chair she sits in for eight hours a day as shackles and her office as a tomb. She can't wait for five o'clock each day so that she can hit the road. The mountains, rivers and lakes are where she wants to be—climbing the highest peaks, rafting the wildest rapids and swimming the clearest lakes. Exploration and Endurance are sure to be at least two of this woman's motivational factors, and the keys to her happiness.

A lawyer gets to the office early every day with a smile on his face. He always has a fresh pot of coffee ready for the rest of the office personnel. He works long hours and is determined to do his best for both the clients and the law firm. He happily takes on more than his share of cases, and he always has a smile on his face. It is easy to surmise that Achievement and Passion are on this man's list of motivational factors. Fulfillment for him comes from his professional achievements.

Knowing what core motivational factors unlock your own happiness is the key to finding life success. You can do any job or have any career that makes money, but if you are not doing something that satisfies your inner core, you will never be truly happy and fulfilled. Knowing what makes you happy, and how you want to live, are the fundamental ingredients for achieving your life success.

David Michael Ferruolo

-Exercise 3A-

What Makes You Happy?

Think about those things that put a smile on your face. In the moments when you are living in total bliss, what are you doing? Who are you with? What are your surroundings? What are the circumstances that make you happy? Describe those moments below, in any order, in as much detail as possible.

_____

_____

_____

_____

_____

_____

_____

_____

_____

_____

Elements of Life Success

David Michael Ferruolo

-Exercise 3B-

Your Motivational Factors

Read over what you have written in the above exercise, and try to determine what really makes you tick. What are your core values? What motivational factors are at the root of your actions? Then make a list of all the relevant motivational factors, and circle the one or two that drive you most deeply.

David Michael Ferruolo

Elements of Life Success

David Michael Ferruolo

-Chapter 4-

What Are You Made Of?

I strongly believe people are capable of doing amazing things and making their dreams a reality, as long as they have a positive attitude, a good plan and are not afraid of a little hard work.

Finding your motivational factors and what makes you happy is a very important first step in creating a successful life. It is also imperative to know what you are physically, emotionally and mentally capable of. Defining your God-given attributes will help you make the right decisions about the life you can lead. This is not meant to limit you, but rather to empower you to look at avenues worthy of your pursuit and not waste precious time with ventures that realistically are beyond your capabilities.

This process can be very difficult, because it sometimes is hard to tell the difference between a limiting attribute and a potential capability. For instance, I nearly failed English while in high school and was told by several teachers that I was not college material. So I went into the military instead. Years later, not satisfied with my military career, I began to question the advice I had received during my senior year of high school. I decided to give college a try and ended up making the Dean's list over and over again. Funny, I also aced my English classes. This is a prime example of unexplored potential. Now, I did have a fallback plan. If I had gone to college after the military and not done well or was unhappy, my plan was to reenlist and make a career out of service to my country. But thank God I took that chance to find out—now I do serve, but in a much different way!

Sometimes it only takes a bit of exploration to know if you have a limiting factor or a hidden potential to excel. Either way, the information is good to know. There are really no endeavors unworthy of effort—all experiences bring us closer to the knowledge of who we really are.

Nevertheless, it is disheartening to see people who are really not capable of certain things keep trying to make them happen over and over again. The pain they cause themselves, their friends, their family is unhealthy and unwarranted. If only they could get past their ego misleading them with inflated dreams or their fear of looking like a failure, they could move on and choose to be a success at what they are actually able to do.

I had a customer some time ago at my scuba diving store who wanted to be a diving instructor. He was a really nice guy and everyone liked him. He tried everything to become a good diver, but he was not. He was a danger to himself and others around him. He does not possess the common-sense skills to excel as a recreational sport diver, never mind being a certified instructor. For years he kept diving, skirting bad incidents over and over again, in hopes of developing the skills to teach diving someday. I tried to let him know how much work it was going to be and to advise him of the cost of becoming certified to teach. Nothing I did or said deterred him from trying.

Finally, when one day he became forceful about me certifying him, I had to tell him honestly my professional opinion of his skills. I let him know that for the safety of my students, there was no way he would ever be a diving instructor with my company and that he should get it out of his mind. Well, he cursed me and vowed to find someone else who would make him an instructor. He does not come into my shop anymore, and to the best of my knowledge nobody else has allowed him to teach either!

Examples of limiting factors would include: being only 5'4" tall and wanting to play professional basketball; having poor eyesight and trying to fly jets in the Air Force; being tone deaf and auditioning for a lead singer position. These are extreme examples, but I have seen them all. People who just can't teach continue to teach; shy and introverted people try to be salespeople; clumsy and uncoordinated people pursue athletic activities; people with no technical aptitude try to work with computers. The list goes on and on. And although kudos may be warranted for the tremendous effort some of these people put forth, the pain and frustration they experience do not seem worth the exertion. If the same efforts were put into occupations and tasks more congruent with their attributes, their potential would be limitless, and much more fulfilling.

It is easier to know what you are good at than what you cannot do. Most of us have an idea of our talents and attributes, but we were never taught to link these abilities with what makes us happy and to search for a career that encompasses both. When we are able to put these three pieces of the success puzzle together, we will be able to excel in life and be fulfilled and happy at the same time.

Many years back, I used to do some side work for a friend who owned a roofing and remodeling business. He had one employee whom we both called "The Dude." He was a reliable employee and did good work, but my friend always was after him to work harder and faster. "The Dude" never really complained, but I knew he disliked this work tremendously. What he did like was to rock climb, mountain bike and backpack. He was a talented climber and seemed to enjoy the challenge of negotiating a demanding headwall. I always believed he was bright and capable, but he never seemed to be able to get his life in order.

After several years of doing construction and roofing, he moved on to work for a paving company owned by another long-time friend of mine. There he worked hard and was appreciated by management and coworkers, but still he was not content. When I saw my friend, he told me "The Dude" was a great worker, but he also knew he was destined for something else.

Years later, a patron walked into my store and said, "Hey, Dave." I vaguely recognized the voice and could not place the face for a few moments. Then I realized who it was—"The Dude"—10 years later. Our conversation revealed that he had gone into law enforcement and had a talent for it. He was picked for the regional SWAT team, and other officers I know there say he is one of their better operating team members. I had to laugh. How could someone who was so affectionately called "The Dude" excel on a SWAT team? On top of that, he was now married and had several children. I was bemused.

Well, "The Dude" became "The Man" when he realized that a career in law enforcement could combine his innate talents with what intrinsically made him happy.

It may take you some time and lots of figuring to put all the pieces together, but since there are only really three parts to the puzzle, you can and should give it a try. If you are not happy with your current place in life, or if you feel you should be doing something else, then you need to take the time to find out what you are capable of doing that will make you happy at the same time. I truly believe we all have an inkling of what we could do and what would make us happy. Sometimes those thoughts stay with us for years. It is up to us to decide to follow our hearts or accept a mediocre existence.

Recently I got reacquainted with a classmate from high school. I had not seen this person for about 20 years. When I asked what she was doing for a living, she frowned and said she was in transition. I replied what a good thing that was, and that most people would never, at 39 years old, venture to change careers. She described how she finally decided to follow her dream of being a nurse, after thinking about it most of her adult life. After a long time, she realized that she had the skills, aptitude and determination to make the change. I'm very confident that, within a few years, she'll have a position at the local hospital.

When we know what we are able to do and when we can define those attributes, skills and talents that make us special, we can put all three pieces of the puzzle together and find a career that will be fulfilling.

-Exercise 4-

What Are You Good At?

So what are you best at? What are those hidden and not-so-hidden talents and attributes you possess? Are you creative? Analytical? Are you good with people? Can you tell a great story? Are you extremely strong and athletic? Do you excel intellectually? Can you paint, or are you good at math? Can you fix anything, or are you talented at visualizing new concepts? Can you write, build homes, run a family or a country? What makes you special? What sets you apart from others?

If you are not sure what you are good at, write about the thoughts that have recurred in your mind over the years about what you might like to do with your life.

Take some time to think about these questions. When you are ready, write it all down here:

David Michael Ferruolo

Elements of Life Success

David Michael Ferruolo

-Chapter 5-

Putting It All Together

I thought about baking a cake a few months ago, so I rummaged through the pantry to find what I thought should be in a cake. I haphazardly mixed my bizarre concoction in a big bowl, and as I looked at it, I thought that somehow it did not have the right "cake-like" consistency about it. Oh well, I thought, I'm sure it will be just fine.

I poured the batter in the baking pan and popped it in the oven. I wondered how long I should bake it, so I went on the Internet looking for cake baking times. There I found a lot of really good recipes, which told me not only how long to bake it but also what should go into the batter and how to mix it all together.

Looking over some of these great formulas for scrumptious cakes, I started to think that maybe I had done a few things wrong. Just at that time the buzzer on the oven sounded, and I happily went to see my great creation. The smell was certainly alluring as I opened the oven door, but the look was far from what I expected. It appeared more like a boiling mass of brown sticky lava than an edible dessert.

I then thought about the irony of it all. If I can't even wing baking a cake, how on earth can I possibly live my life by the seat of my pants? I knew then that I needed a plan, a recipe—a formula for what I want to do and how I want to live my life.

In the preceding two chapters we discussed how to find some of the essential elements of life success. Knowing what makes us happy, how we want to live our lives and what attributes and characters we possess are the key ingredients for that formula. Once we have all the necessary parts, we can proceed to mix it all up and finally begin to envision what will fulfill our lives and souls.

So now that we have taken the time to find the pieces of our success puzzle, it's time to put it all together and see what it looks like. When you begin to do this, when you finally have a direction to pursue in your life, a miraculous thing will happen to you. When you are freed of the frustration of knowing you are meant for a different purpose in life, and when you can finally see and know your destiny, your spirit awakens and you are inspired to take the action to make your dreams a reality.

Care must be taken, however, when fitting the pieces together. This is a delicate balance of what you like, how you want to live and what you are capable of. If the mix is too much of one thing or too little of another, the puzzle may not fit exactly together, and the recipe may turn out to be a mess rather than a cake. Make sure you take the time to really think about what you have to work with and what you can do with it. That is what we are trying to figure out in this chapter: What can you do with your life that will encompass all the pieces of your puzzle? When we mix all the proper ingredients up and bake it—what jobs, careers, hobbies and lifestyles will rise when the buzzer goes off? What is your recipe, and what will be the results?

Sometimes this is very hard to figure out, and we need some outside help. Family and friends can sometimes shed some light, but they may be too close to you and not objective enough to see the entire picture of what you are trying to do. Sometimes it is wise to enlist the help of a co-worker, business associate or acquaintance who is willing to listen and help. An outside view by someone who is a bit removed from your circle of friends may be less skewed by their past relations with you or their deep feelings towards you. In fact, this may be a good time to get the help of a professional career counselor or a life coach.

It is important to get some outside input—and you should listen to everyone. Wisdom comes in many ways, in many forms and from many sources. Once you have enough input, start sifting through it to determine what should be your true path. Remember that you must make the final decision. The right choice comes from you. You will feel it—you will know. Don't be swayed towards doing something someone else suggests if you do not resonate with it, if you do not feel it in your heart.

Ultimately, the puzzle of your life success is yours alone to figure out. Suggestions and help should always be welcome, but you must lay the final pieces and make the final decisions on your own.

It took me years of hard work and determination to build my business and make a decent life for myself. And although things were going well enough for me, I was unsatisfied and frustrated with my place in life. One day I sat down and took an inventory of my life to find out what sorts of things really made me happy. After a few days of thinking about it, I had a good list of the things that always make my life happy. My list consisted of items such as:

- *I enjoy working from home so my son can be with me all day.*
- *I love to perform. There's nothing quite like being on stage in front of an audience.*
- *I love adventure and travel. Experiencing new places and new things is exhilarating.*
- *I have a passion for philosophy and metaphysics. I could read about these subjects all day.*
- *I like being around people in a leader or instructor capacity. I enjoy teaching and helping people, and I get joy from seeing them achieve their goals.*
- *I thrive on being outside in nature – hiking, kayaking, skiing, scuba diving.*
- *I love being creative and dreaming up new concepts or new ways to do things. For fun I come up with new business plans or marketing ideas for friends and for myself.*
- *I love playing and listening to music. I really enjoy live band performances.*
- *I like the finer things in life, and I appreciate the value of high quality in items like vehicles, guitars, appliances, clothes and computers. I go for specialty services like gourmet restaurants, top-notch vacation properties and salon-quality haircuts.*

I thought about my list for a while and realized I've had or now have almost all the items on the list, but not at the same time. The Navy offered lots of travel and adventure, but although I was outside often, it did not fulfill much else on the list. Being in college and playing full-time in bands was very close to my nirvana, but I was always broke and struggling for my next meal. My current diving business provides a good paycheck and the opportunity to teach scuba diving, travel during the off-season and work outside. But still, it lacks many other pieces of the puzzle.

I decided it might be a good idea to pinpoint where my talents lay. What were my best attributes? I thought this could shed some light on what I should do to bring more enjoyment into my life. My attribute list looked like this:

- *I'm a visionary, able to see something great from nothing and all the steps to get there.*
- *I'm very creative and can easily come up with new ways to do things or improve old ideas.*
- *I'm a natural leader and teacher.*
- *I'm extremely articulate, have good stage presence and am a captivating storyteller.*
- *I'm able to simplify abstract concepts and difficult ideas into easy-to-understand verbiage.*
- *I have incredible mental and physical stamina, and I seem to have an unlimited amount of energy.*
- *Because of my thirst for reading, learning and experiencing new things all the time, I know a lot about a multitude of subjects.*
- *People are naturally drawn to me, and I have the ability to inspire them.*

Yet this second list did not bring me any closer to finding out who I was and what I wanted to do with my life, much less actually make me excited to get out of bed every day. At first it seemed that I was no nearer a breakthrough than I was before. For a while, I accepted my frustrating, unfulfilled life just the way it was. I focused on looking for my bliss within that life, and for most of that year I kept a journal to document my road to self-love and happiness.

During this time, I routinely shared my thoughts with close friends and sometimes with scuba students. Each time, I got the same response: people loved it and always wanted to hear more. It was about that time in my life that I met some people who thought I should write a book about my life and become a professional motivational speaker. I immediately dismissed the idea as ludicrous.

A few weeks later, I pondered my two lists simultaneously. I was amazed at what I saw. If I were to become an author and speaker, as those people had suggested, it would satisfy every item on my lists. As this thought sank in, I sensed a power radiating within and energizing me. It felt as if I could somehow jump out of my chair and fly to the heavens. Unexpectedly, tears came to my eyes and I felt as if I had wings. Suddenly the possibilities in my life were endless. For the first time, my body, mind and spirit seemed to be one—I was complete with the knowledge of what my life path should be.

It is said that when you find your life path—your purpose for living—the universe opens all necessary doors, and the path is illuminated for easy travel. I am a believer, because in less than one year from that day, my first book, *Connecting with the Bliss of Life*, was published.

It is my sincere hope that you find your purpose and live your blissful life of success. It is time now to take your lists and start brainstorming about the possibilities. By mixing the right ingredients together, what will the finished product look like? By fitting all the pieces of the puzzle correctly, what does the picture tell you? You may be very surprised to find out that you have already thought of this path long ago, but somehow you took a wrong turn and lost your way. I know that over 15 years before I started writing *Connecting with the Bliss of Life*; I considered becoming a motivational speaker. I did take a significant detour, but I eventually found my way home. So it took a decade and a half—better late than never! And it's never too late—never!

-Exercise 5A-

Brainstorming the Possibilities

Using your "happiness" list and your "capabilities" list, imagine the possibilities of what you can do with your life that would satisfy all the things on both your lists.

Be creative and think outside the box. I never in my life imagined I would ever publish a book, but this is now my second and I have several others on the way. Do not limit your thinking—let your aspirations run wild. On this list, anything goes—write down as many ideas as possible.

Elements of Life Success

-Exercise 5B-

Honing It Down

Now look over your list and find the things that not only excite you but also that you know can be accomplished and that you can do. You may end up with one or several items on this list, but they should all be things you can see yourself doing for the rest of your life. For each of these items—and try to make it no more than three—write why you know each path can be accomplished and what will be the benefits to your life when you are living your dreams.

Elements of Life Success

David Michael Ferruolo

-Chapter 6-

Thought: The Hidden Power To Make or Break You

Anyone can have creative, lofty dreams and desires, but without a positive mindset it is nearly impossible to succeed. Our thoughts are like directional signposts embedded in our subconscious minds. Whatever our mental disposition, negative or positive, we seem to always find ourselves surrounded by circumstances or situations that mirror out thoughts. We have an unconscious tendency to actively seek out situations and outcomes that are congruent with our predisposed mindset.

Think of our inner thought-dialogue as a map of the highways of life and our body as a humble vehicle. When we encounter a situation that requires an important decision, our mind reads the map of its inner voice and dictates the choice to be made. The outcome of our choice depends on whether we are predisposed toward a negative or positive thought process regarding that particular situation.

We truly do not know what we are made of or what we are capable of until we are faced with decisions that affect our lives. By looking at how we react in different situations, we can see if we are optimistic about life or not.

For instance, if you have a negative predisposition toward romantic possibilities and think that every time you meet someone it will end quickly with a painful result, inevitably you will choose someone to date who will fulfill what you think. Similarly, if things are going well at first, you will subconsciously create circumstances that will bring about your romance's demise.

It is all too common for people to create outer situations to reflect their inner thought processes, and it can happen in all areas of life. Most of the time people will be unaware of their unconscious-based behaviors and unknowingly react out of habit. This type of response to a situation is sometimes classified as reactionary behavior. When we habitually take action without awareness or intellectual input, we are being reactionary to our situations. Unfortunately, letting our unconscious fears and insecurities dictate our responses will only bring more hardship and pain into our lives.

I use to pride myself on my intelligence and my abilities. In conversation, I was pompous and cocky. I would always say it was because I was so confident that I acted this way, and that people just did not understand. After all, I'm a former Navy SEAL! What do they know, right? But my true nature, my true intellect and abilities, were always masked by my need to be the best. This often caused difficulties in my life and business.

David Michael Ferruolo

I would routinely get into arguments with friends and customers. I would yell at employees and students. What was *their* problem anyway? Any time someone would question my abilities in any way, I would react with anger and spite. I would make sure they knew how wrong they were and that I was right. I was rude, forceful and hurtful. Little did I know how insecure I really was. I would take action without awareness or intellectual input. I was reactionary and therefore let my unconscious fears and insecurities dictate my responses.

True intellect and strength come from being humble and seeking to see another's point of view. Greatness is subtle and kind, not loud and forceful. When I finally weeded those pesky negative thoughts and insecurities from my mind, I had a much better outlook on life. I was able to think more clearly and take the appropriate actions to create better circumstances for myself and for everyone around me.

So, then, our mission of making our dreams come true is twofold: first, to reprogram our mindset to be optimistic and positive, and second, to train ourselves to be proactive when making decisions. Once the script in our heads has been rewritten to reflect optimism and zeal, we will automatically make the correct choices in the best interests of everyone involved. However, we must always circumvent negative thoughts and destructive tendencies by actively and intelligently reviewing the circumstances and the possible outcomes before we react.

Part of my business is placing mooring systems for boats into a large lake. A mooring system consists of a 1,000- or 500-pound concrete block, heavy chain, float buoy and a line to attach the boat to the chain. Moorings are much safer than docks in bad, windy weather.

I have a 26'x10' steel barge that I use to transport the heavy blocks of concrete and other materials across the lake to customers' lakefront homes. Due to the material and labor costs associated with installation, mooring fields can be very expensive.

I had negotiated a contract with a certain housing association for six new moorings. After the contract had been signed, the president of the association called to get me to drop the price again. I had already cut the price significantly. I agreed to the new price, on the condition that I could cut out some of the extra side work I had in the original contract. He faxed back the same contract to my office with the new price on it and initialed the change. I was on my cell phone at the time away from the office, so I did not have the opportunity to review the contract—and I did not think I needed to.

The next day I showed up at the property in a great mood and ready to install their mooring field to my usual high standards. But trouble lurked in the form of a canoe with two men in it. They came alongside the barge to inspect the materials and to make sure I was going to do everything I had stated in the contract. I told them that due to the new reduced price, I would not be removing the old materials or moving their raft over, confirming what I had said on the phone. The association president held up the contract and said that I had to abide to it as written, or I could go home and return his full deposit.

David Michael Ferruolo

This was not an option, because I already had several thousand dollars invested in this project. We got into an argument and started to yell at each other. My blood was boiling, and I felt the rage building up inside me. I was inches from the edge of my barge, and I knelt over and said, "Do you really want to piss off a former Navy SEAL?" I looked back at my friend Mark, who was helping me for the day, and gave him a devilish smirk. I took off my sunglasses and was just about to jump off the barge and flip the canoe over.

What fun that would have been! But I caught myself just in time. Is this who I want to be? Is this how I want to be known? Is this who I really am? No, I thought. I'm better than the very visibly angry men in the canoe. I closed my eyes and caught my breath. I looked at the contract and smiled. All at once, I changed my attitude and happily said, "Okay. I'll do it. Just as it is written on the contract. Sorry for the confusion. Now please move away so your canoe does not flip as we place the blocks in the water."

Both men in the canoe were confused. The president asked, "You'll do it all? As written in the contract?" I replied happily, "Sure," and I placed their mooring field to the best of my ability. I felt great for having the strength to suck it up. I might not have made the money I needed to on that job, but I felt very powerful. I kept an optimistic outlook and concentrated on doing great work. I was in a good mood again, and it remained with me for the rest of the day. I learned much about myself and my commitment to being the best person I can be. I also learned how my thoughts could shape my mood and alter a situation.

So, you see, our thoughts play a powerful role in shaping our reality. Are you an optimist or pessimist? Is your glass half full or half empty? The optimists in life always seem to see the best in every situation and somehow always come out on top. Even in the face of failure, optimists will understand the lesson and use the knowledge to catapult themselves into other positive directions. The pessimists, on the other hand, look for all the ways to fail before they start. And when things fall apart, as they always do, the pessimists will say, "I told you it wouldn't work," and angrily retreat into the old, habitually negative way of life they were trying to get away from.

Optimists are forever in motion, thinking, creating and achieving, while pessimists are stale and stagnant. A positive, proactive person is always full of energy and zest and seems to be happy and content with life at all times. Conversely, the pessimist tends to be dismal, in despair, and has the same worn-out complaints year after year.

If you find yourself in the latter category, don't feel ashamed or guilty. These states of mind are *choices*. You really can choose to change, and since the world as we know it is really perceived from our inner screen of thought, we can create an optimistic, positive reality instead of a negative reality, just by choosing to do so. In his book, *The Power of Intention,* Dr. Wayne Dyer writes; "If you change the way you look at things, the things you look at change." Simply put, if we choose to see the world as an oyster containing all our dreams and desires, it will become that.

Concentrate on changing the dialogue in your mind to reflect optimism, enthusiasm and confidence. Program your mind to see the best in all situations, for all circumstances do have a positive side. You just have to look for it. Affirm to yourself daily: "Things are going well, and I am on the right path." Know that you have it in you to create you life and fulfill your dreams and desires. Watch you thoughts and train yourself to concentrate only on what you wish to bring into your life and not what you are trying to avoid. Stay positive and optimistic and watch the reality of your world change before your eyes. The results will amaze you!

-Exercise 6-

Change the Way You Look at Things

Write about a negative life situation that has been bothering you. Then look hard for the positive sides of it – this may be difficult, but try to be creative – and see if you can come up with a more positive viewpoint:

Elements of Life Success

David Michael Ferruolo

-Chapter 7-

Scripting Your Life

It's sometimes hard to know what we want to do with our lives until we understand our motivational factors and evaluate our personal skills and attributes. Once we know what drives us, and what we can do physically and mentally, we can get a better handle on what makes us happy and fulfilled. This knowledge is instrumental in deciding which paths we take in life. Still, the vastness of opportunities available to us can make it confusing, even overwhelming, to know which road to choose. But it may help to know this: *There are as many avenues to prosperity and fulfillment as there are to dissonance and despair.*

If you understand what drives you and trust your instincts, you will find the one right path for you. Some kind of movement, however, is of the utmost importance. If you don't know what to do, do something—anything. A body in motion will find more opportunities for action, and may be propelled in several interesting directions, while the motionless body sits stagnant. That's why the best tennis players, the best baseball hitters, and the best football quarterbacks and receivers learn to stay in motion while waiting for the perfect opportunity to score.

Just do not sit around and be dormant. If you can find no direction and still feel you should wait, then do not sit vegetating the house. Get out, go for a drive, take a walk, or find a bookstore and just browse the aisles. Gather information on several topics. Research, learn and expand your base of knowledge. This is motion, and none of it will be wasted.

After my first book, *Connected with the Bliss of Life,* was published, I had a thousand copies sitting at the foot of my bed waiting to be sold. I felt the burning need to market and promote it. I was driving myself crazy thinking of what the next step could or should be. I had worked long and hard to get to that point, and yet I knew I had to just let things happen—to blossom. I had done all the work, taken all the right steps, and now the ball was in the court of others—the reviewers, the book buyers, the staff at Amazon.com and my promotional agent Cate Cummings. I knew I had done all I could, yet I still felt frustrated and on the brink of breakdown. I was not adhering to the philosophies of my own writing, and the result was stress.

Luckily, my good friend Jennifer offered some excellent advice. She suggested that I take a day and do nothing. She recommended that I go to the mall and just hang out at the bookstore. Great idea, I thought, and off I went to EMS and Borders. As I drove down the highway my mood elevated. It was such a beautiful day, and I was happy not to be at work.

I found a great new hiking shirt and new boots at EMS, and my bookstore time was even more productive. I spent about two hours researching the self-help and spirituality sections of the store for the different new books being offered. I learned a lot about what people are reading and what is actually being sold. I had a good day doing "nothing" but gained something positive from it. Not only did I have some new clothes, I had a great idea for my next book and even knew how long and what price it should be.

So, if you do not know where to go, just go somewhere. Sometimes your subconscious will guide you to where you need to be. You never know where you may end up, and it could be life-changing. This is a great strategy, and I have used it many times with tremendous success.

However, having a plan or even a general idea of how you want to live will allow you to travel faster down the road of creating your successful life. Couple this "Do Anything" technique with your motivational factors, and you will have a foundation for decision-making when faced with life's tougher questions. Even more useful is to try working backward. One of the dictums in business planning is always to start with the end in mind. But for this, you need to have a clear idea of what the end looks like.

The most powerful process I've developed to discern what I wish for my life is one I call *"Scripting Your Life."* It is the simple yet potent and emotional process of writing down the story of your life, but from the perspective of being *at the end of your life*. You would start your story from today, where you are right now, and write a script for the rest of your life as if it is happening from this point on.

You could choose a different outcome for every day, but you should choose the outcome before you begin to write.

I first thought of this process when visiting my grandfather while he was living in a nursing home. I would visit frequently before he died, and as I spoke with the many other guests at the home, I started to hear the same story over and over. It was always very similar: "If only I could do it all over again. If I could be 25 again, I'd do it differently." I never heard anyone say that they would make a million dollars or that they would spend more time at the office. But I did hear things like: "I'd travel more" or "I'd spend more time with my kids and family" or "I'd learn to play a musical instrument." Many answers were tinged with regret: "I would have taken more chances" or "I would have been less angry" or "I would have forgiven my parents."

Mostly, these elderly people talked about how they would just live a more loving and fulfilling life. I always wondered what they would actually do if they could be 25 again. Would they indeed live life to the fullest? My guess is that they would try.

But what do these stories tell us about ourselves? We who still have the chance to seize the moment should do so! We can change right now, and the process of scripting your life can greatly help you define how you would like to live. Take this process very seriously. Do it over time. Do not rush it or be haphazard. The exercise is simple but very powerful if you put time and energy into it.

How do you begin scripting your life? Imagine yourself to be very old with only a few months left to live. Now you are sitting quietly in your home. You know that the end is near, and you are looking back and reflecting on your life. Consider every choice, every accomplishment, and every adventure. But you have the power to do things differently this time. Script your life as if you had lived it to the fullest. You successfully met all adversity and all challenges with optimism. You faced your fears, and you moved beyond your doubts. You were loving and giving, and you lived in harmony and peace with yourself, others and the world. You were respectful and highly respected.

What did your life look like? You fill in the blanks, the places, the people, the careers and the travels. Write it all down. How would you like the story of your life to read? Write the script of your life exactly as you would wish to live the rest of your life. Now sit back and think for a moment. Take a deep breath. Inhale the essence of your life. Close your eyes and imagine that you were able to create this amazing life and that you actually lived the life of your dreams.

How does this feel, deep inside, knowing that you accomplished all you set out to do? Knowing that you lived an inspirational, magical, fairy-tale life? How do you feel knowing you attained everything in your life that you dreamed and desired? Imagine, as you sit in quiet contemplation and review your remarkable life, that you can peacefully and gracefully accept death now because you know that you have done everything you wanted to do while alive. You know that when your time comes, you are ready to go. How does this feel? In your body? In your heart? Allow yourself time to feel it all for a few moments.

Elements of Life Success

Now let's change it around a little bit and rewrite the script. What if you never did *anything* you desired? What if you have only a few months to live and are too feeble to do anything else? As you look back on your life, you see only the wasted time and missed opportunities. You lived your entire life in fear or in anger. You let precious seconds of your life slip away like sand through your fingertips, and now it is too late—the game is over. How do you feel now?

If you have the choice of either script to live, which would it be? Knowing that both stories end with your death, why not choose to live on fire? Why not choose to face life with enthusiasm and anticipation, knowing the remarkable adventure your life could be? The script is yours to write. How do you want to look back on your life at the very end of it? It's your choice.

David Michael Ferruolo

-Exercise 5-

Scripting Your Life

Write the script of your life exactly as you wish to live the rest of your time on earth. If you need more space, use a journal or a notebook.

David Michael Ferruolo

David Michael Ferruolo

-Chapter 8-

Deciding to Fly

How does a bird know it can fly? Well, it doesn't until it jumps out of the tree and spreads its wings. Sure, it has seen other birds fly, but it has never known flight itself. How can it truly be sure it will be able to fly or if it is ready? Perhaps there is a knowing deep within its being that flight is its purpose, or maybe it feels it can do what others of its kind are doing? Whatever the reason, one thing remains true: A bird takes flight regardless of the uncertainty of the outcome. It feels it, it knows it, and nothing will keep it from attempting that first flight.

A bird is blessed with wings and the instinct to know how to use them. It doesn't doubt its ability or its purpose. It just takes that blind leap of faith and flies. And yes, there is that chance it will fall straight to the ground. Yet it eagerly jumps out of the nest. Just think of what nature would be like if the bird were afraid to fly, the fish petrified to swim, or the lion hesitant to roar. If humans are the dominant species on this planet, why do so many of us deny our abilities and instincts, doubting our purpose and what we are capable of? Why are we the only beings on the planet afraid to take that leap of faith? Human capabilities are almost limitless. We were born to create; we were born for adventure; and we were born for success. What makes us stand at the edge of our dreams, rooted in fear and insecurity? Denying our God-given capabilities and characters is a sin—a sin punishable by a lifetime of misery.

No one would dispute the wonder of the human body, but our most important asset is the human mind. We possess an intelligence that surpasses all other beings on our planet. When effort and determination are applied, the human mind and body have unlimited capabilities. Think of all the amazing things humans have created. Look around you. So many "everyday items" that we take for granted are amazingly creative: cell phones, computers, televisions, or even simple things like shoes, screwdrivers, Velcro, or, hey, even the pen and paper. What other creature on earth can boast such powers of invention? Now, look at all the places humans have gone. We've ascended our highest and most rugged mountains, dived the depths of our vast oceans, and even orbited the earth and walked on the moon!

No other species on this earth could survive such diverse environments. Humans are the most amazing creations on the planet, blessed with limitless capabilities and infinite possibilities. Like our friend the bird, humans know deep within their beings what they are capable of. They see other humans creating, inventing and accomplishing. However, when the bird is ready, it takes that leap of faith, spreads it wings, and soars through the skies. When humans are ready to leave their nests, they often choose to accept old limits and live by standards unworthy of their amazing minds and bodies.

Being on the Navy SEAL teams really opened my mind to the amazing potential of the human mind and body. The acronym SEAL stands for Sea, Air and Land, which means the units are capable of attack or insertion from all angles—high, low and straight on. We are all qualified for both scuba diving and skydiving. We operate in cold climates on skis and snowshoes, and in the desert or jungle trekking on foot. We train to swim oceans and climb mountains. There is no territory on earth in which a SEAL unit cannot operate.

Every member in my 16-man platoon had a very distinct personality, but we all shared one similar trait: We accepted no limitations to what we could accomplish. We somehow were all able to move beyond fear and insecurity, venture into new territories with excitement, and accomplish what most people would consider undoable or just plain insane. This is because we all focused on the possibilities and not the obstacles. We were all incredibly creative problem solvers, and when the going got tough, we got tougher. Our mindset made the difference that enabled us to do all those "crazy" things.

All humans possess a superior cognitive ability that separates us from the animals and gives us wondrous creativity to invent and solve problems. It is ironic, then, that our cognitive ability can be the pathway for both our inspiration and our downfall. As easily as we can create a mental platform of unrestricted flight for our existence, we can create a gloomy dungeon in which to wallow and waste our lives. Our minds are capable of great illusions that can serve either as our wings or our chains, depending on our chosen mindset.

When we have a mental program of hope, optimism and achievement, our potential is limitless. However, when we have an attitude laden with cynical and pessimistic thought processes, we end up with a dissonant, sorrowful existence instead. Negative past experiences and pessimistic social conditioning can produce these self-destructive mindsets, and fear is the overall result, whether it be fear of the past or fear of the future.

Many books have been written about overcoming fears, but I will give you the no-nonsense, nuts-and-bolts explanation that I feel is most important. As I see it, most people are either afraid of the failures of the past or afraid of the uncertainties of the future – or a bit of both. I will tell you that past performances do not predict future results! What has happened to you in the past absolutely does not mean it will continue to occur in the future. If you cling to a pessimistic, negative mindset, you may in fact create situations that are similar to the past. You will unconsciously create a negative situation, just so you can be right. But you can just as easily adopt a positive mindset and open up a whole new future for yourself. The simple truth is that the past does not exist except within the confines of the mind.

When we give too much energy to past negative situations in the form of continual thought, it becomes our view of how things should be and will always be. We create a fictional reality in our minds that tells us everything will always turn out the same way it has in the past. Our mind is so fixated on the negative outcomes that we actually seek them out to fulfill our vision. Whether consciously or not, we sabotage our situations in order to have things turn out poorly. When living with the fears of the past, we allow ourselves to be resigned about the present and accept mediocrity as the norm for life. We live shackled to the thoughts of everything ending badly, so we either give new ventures a half-baked attempt or never try them at all, not expecting that anything grand could come of our efforts.

The past is only a memory, and it can't do you any harm unless you allow it to. Your actions and the current situation in which you are living right now are the only defining realities you have. If you are not in physical danger or pain right now, then you are okay. Now is the time you live in, not the past. Turn off the re-run movie in your head and replace it with a scenario of empowerment and accomplishment.

Like the past, the future does not exist. It is still unwritten and completely uncertain. It has not yet happened, so what is there to fear? Is it intelligent to fear hypothetical scenes or made-up fantasies? No one can predict or control the future; it is completely unwritten and unknown. What you do *now* will determine your future. So spend more time thinking about your well-being in the now, in this moment. Do not concern yourself with the details of what may or may not happen sometime, someday. Be okay right now, and carry that feeling forward with each tick of the clock. And, if you do find yourself in a dangerous, fearful situation, act accordingly with intelligence, but act in and for that moment, not in fear of the past or future.

Franklin D. Roosevelt said, "The only thing we have to fear is fear itself." This statement is so profoundly true. We should not fear living life; we should be afraid of fear only because fear can keep us from taking action and truly living. If the bird were consumed with fear, it would never take action and realize it could fly. What a miserable life that bird would have if it denied its spirit and never left the nest! Know that fear is illusionary and self-generated. It is in your being to live life to the fullest. Deciding to take the chance, deciding to spread your wings, deciding to take that leap of faith into the unknown is one of the hardest but most powerful decisions you can make.

And really, why not just give it a shot? Would you be better off not trying? And what if... what if you did turn your dreams into reality?

-Exercise 8-

Overcoming Your Fears

Write a motivational letter to yourself, explaining all the reasons you should give up your fears and put more effort into living a more rewarding life by going after your dreams.

David Michael Ferruolo

David Michael Ferruolo

-Chapter 9-

The Importance of Goals

    A dream becomes a goal when it is written down on paper. The goal becomes a series of steps. There is a tremendous power that comes from seeing what you want to do with your life in writing. Goals create a solid foundation for the decisions that you make on a daily basis. Life has so many variations and choices that your decisions about what you do are limitless. By having concrete, written and memorized goals, you'll have the ability to better choose your daily path and be closer to attaining what you want. Think of your goals as destinations on a map and the steps of your goals as the routes that you are planning to take to reach your destination.

    If you lived in Boston, Massachusetts, and you wanted to move somewhere that was warm year-round, it would be inefficient just to get in your car with all your stuff and drive aimlessly around the country until you found sunshine. In fact, if you don't have the correct, planned route in mind, you might never find what you are looking for. However, if you do some research and decide to pick San Diego, California, as your final destination and choose routes on the map, you will have a solid foundation to plan your trip so that you can reach your destination in a safe and timely manner. Every time you come to an intersection along the way, you'll know which direction to go. When the signpost reads "North to Idaho, South to Texas, West to California," you'll know that you need to drive west because you have already made your map. We might also call this map your action plan. You cannot construct an action plan without a definite destination in mind. Your goals are your waypoints in life; they are your wants, dreams and desires. Once written down, your goals become your tools of empowerment. You now have a guide for intelligent decision-making, so you know what actions to take next.

An intelligent decision is a choice you make that is consistent with your goals and your life plan. Making more intelligent life choices that are in concert with your goals will bring you closer to what you want and not farther away from it. In contrast, facing important life decisions without well-defined goals is just like going on that cross-country trip without a map or a destination in mind. Aimlessly driving around in circles, you will become frustrated and angered that you are not really getting anywhere. Spinning your wheels is fine if you're riding a bike, but is not for living a fulfilling life.

To live your life on purpose, with purpose, you have to know where you are going, and you have to have realistic, well-thought-out goals. Setting goals is easier than you may think, and when you really allow yourself to dream your life, it is also a lot of fun.

I like to have five categories of "terms" or time spans for my goals. Setting goals seems much more doable when you break your life down into time segments. If you create a list of overly "lofty" goals, you may feel overwhelmed and think that you'll never be able to accomplish them all. However, if you think in blocks of years and then divide the years into blocks of terms, suddenly it will look much easier to accomplish your aims because they will appear in smaller pieces or steps. Baby steps and proper planning will greatly help you attain everything you want. Here is a list of suggested categories for your term goals:

Immediate
6 months to 1 year goals

Short-Term
2 to 3 year goals

Mid-Term
4 to 6 year goals

Long-Term
7 to 10 year goals

Extended-Range
11 to 15+ year goals

Then, I take each of my term goal categories, and I break down my list of wants and desires into four subcategories. Each of these categories targets a specific area of my life (see below). That makes it much easier to track my progress, and it becomes easier for me to see how I can achieve my goals. I can track my progress for each category of goal separately, and then make quick and effective changes a little at a time. This is much easier than facing a huge list of to-dos on a single page (or several!). Here are the subcategories I have found most useful:

Career Goals
Personal Goals
Family Goals
Lifestyle Goals

Once I have established my goals for each category in each term, I then break them down once more. There are some things I will not sacrifice in this life. Some of these things are mandatory, or "must haves." They may be things I want to do, places I wish to go, items I want to own, or the way I want to look and feel. I also have many things that I feel are not absolutely necessary for me to be happy, but would be like "icing on the cake"—these are the "would be nice" goals. And we all need a few of the loftier goals that I call "dream" goals—the mountain-peak attainments that would make our lives complete. So I break my subcategory goals down this time into the following lists:

"Must Have" Goals
"Would Be Nice" Goals
"Dream" Goals

I do not want to be unrealistic about what I want to attain and do with my life, but I do not want to shortchange myself either. If you shoot for the sun, but end up on the moon, at least you made it to the moon! When creating your list of life goals, make them lofty, but also know where you will be content.

Remember the importance of choosing goals that suit your essence. Traveling down a path that is not congruent with what really makes you happy will only cause you pain and suffering. You may attain some instant or temporary gratification from your achievements, but when the high wears off, you will feel unfulfilled and frustrated. So choose your goals wisely because sometimes you actually get what you go after.

It is very important to have goals, so that you can find direction and purpose in your life. Having well-defined goals can empower you to take action and accomplish what you want to in every aspect of your life. We all have to be careful, however, not to get too attached to the attainment of our goals and forget to live ordinary life along the way. Attachment to your goals can cause much stress and be counterproductive to living a happy life. If you allow your life to focus only on your goals, you will become blind to the power of living in the moment. Every obstacle will seem a disaster, and every setback will cause you to undergo outbursts and breakdowns. You can become consumed with the attainment of the goal and forget to count the daily blessings of your life.

The journey of life is the greatest endeavor there is. It is while traveling our path that our character is formed, lessons are learned, and life is lived. Our goals are only bus stops along the route of life. We will pass through them as quickly as this day is gone. The only time you have to be truly alive is right now, today! So embrace it and live.

The first implicit goal in each of your categories, then, should be to have fun while in the pursuit of your dreams. Do not pass up opportunities to explore other directions. Remember: Goals should not be set in stone; they should have a life of their own. They should evolve and mature just as you do. You should revisit your goals list at least once a year and adapt and revise it as your changing life dictates. As with a cross-country trek, there are many roads that lead to the final destination. Be flexible, yet determined, and remember to have fun along the way.

-Exercise 9-

Have Goals and Have Fun

We must remember while setting our goals and going after our dreams to live life and have fun. Life is about the moments we seize, not where we end up. Actually, we can never really "end up" anywhere in our life because life is always moving forward. Time does not stop when we attain a goal – it moves on – as we should also. Goals are only waypoints along the journey.

First, write a letter of intention to yourself, outlining your commitment to create your goal lists and to follow through with making your dreams a reality. Second, remind yourself that life is an exciting journey to be embraced, and make a solid commitment to have fun while pursuing your dreams. When you are finished, sign and date your letter.

David Michael Ferruolo

David Michael Ferruolo

-Chapter 10-

Set Your Goals

I know what you are thinking – that this process of defining goals requires too much work and wastes too much time, right? Well, you have company. There are a lot of goal gurus out there who profess that goal setting is a quick process of only 30 minutes once a year. But think about that for a moment. If it were that easy to plan out your entire life, wouldn't more people be doing it and attaining what they wanted without any help? Logic tells you then that the gurus probably are underestimating the process. In life, there are no quick fixes or easy ways out. Those who put the effort and time into their lives reap the benefits tenfold. The more time and effort you commit, the larger your rewards will be.

This is reminiscent of Isaac Newton's First Law of Motion, which I have adapted as follows: *"A person at rest tends to stay at rest, and a person in motion tends to stay in motion, at the same pace and in the same recurring situations unless acted upon by inner or outer motivational factors.*" In other words, the effort in equals the rewards out!

So how does that apply to humans and achievement? Simple: If you do not get some form of motivation either internally or externally to do something different with your life, or if you do not exert some effort to change your direction, then you will keep going in the same direction at the same pace forever. So let's be proactive. Let's put some effort into our lives. And let's see what we can achieve and how our lives can blossom. This goal setting and realization process is very powerful, imaginative and fun, so the first rule is to enjoy yourself!

Now that you understand the importance of putting your dreams on paper, we can start turning them into true goals. For this process, you will need a pen or pencil, three different colors of highlighters and a watch or a timer. I suggest that you get out a calendar or your scheduler, so that you can plan the time needed to create comprehensive and concise goal lists. Remember to use the worksheets provided at the end of this chapter to get started.

Creating these goal lists is not a quick process. On average, it takes me a total of 18 to 24 hours to create a comprehensive goal list. And this is a minimum! Depending on the other demands on your time, this process can take as little as one week or as long as two months.

For example, at the minimum, you could spend three to four hours a day for five to seven consecutive days defining your goals for all of the terms and categories we discussed in Chapter 9. Or, at the maximum, you could spend one to two hours for four days a week for four to five weeks. Do not shortchange yourself. It is important to complete each part of the process thoroughly, and to not rush the sessions. Stay focused and stop when you get tired. As you complete the first part of the process, you will have a better idea of your time requirements for the whole project.

When I set goals, I like to work backwards from the desired result to the present when I am setting the goal. It is much easier to break down our term goals into time segments if we know the end result we wish to attain. So, for example, you may want to lose 25 pounds and be able to jog three miles in a half-hour by your next birthday. If your next birthday were seven months away, you would want to break down your weight-loss and running goals into several time segments to track your progress. You may want to set a goal of losing four to five pounds a month. You could start out the first month determined to walk every day. For the second month, you might decide to power-walk, and for the third month, choose to jog a half-mile a few times a week, and so on. If you start with the end in mind, you will be able to plan accurately and have a much better overview of what steps you need to take to achieve your goal.

Extended-Range Goals

Like our San Diego driving directions, we first need to know where we are going before we can create a road map for the trip. So, let's begin with our Extended-Range Goals first. Before we start writing, let's take a few moments to contemplate and visualize what our lives might look like in 15 years. What do you see? What is missing? Add to the picture those things, people, places and events that would make your life complete. Unleash your imagination. Capture the essence of the best and brightest scenario that you can imagine, and let yourself believe that you can accomplish everything you set out to achieve in life.

When you have given yourself adequate time to daydream about the future, and when you are ready to begin outlining your goals, open your Extended-Range Goals to the first page. It should be labeled with the "Career" category. Now, look at your watch or set your timer for six minutes and begin to write. Don't stop to think. Just write as fast as you can without judging what you are writing. Do not worry about penmanship or spelling, just write your heart out. Imagine: If in 15 years you had the perfect career for you, what would it look like? Then write everything you can think about how it would be. Get as detailed as possible. Write as many things as you can in those six minutes. For example, you probably want to include information about your future income, your job title, your co-workers, your office, the number of hours you work, the place you work (e.g., indoors or outdoors), what your typical day involves (even down to your brand of coffee) and how often you travel! Remember: anything and everything you can think of in six minutes – but only six minutes.

At this point, I recommend that you take a break before moving on to the next part of the process. Get some fresh air, grab a snack or have a quick drink of water. Splash some water on your face. Do anything you can to refresh your mind before moving forward. When you are ready to begin again, find your three highlighters and a pen, and grab your newly created Extended-Range Career Goals.

We are now going to rework those goals and break them down into our three subcategories—the "Must Haves," the "Would Be Nices" and the "Dreams."

Take a moment to review your goals while keeping in mind our three subcategories. Look over your list carefully. Consider the following question for each goal on your list: could you be happy and content with something a bit less than what you wrote? The objective here is to find out what the bottom line is for your best possible outcome. Do not try to make your goals less ambitious, but define closely what would fulfill your heart. Do not forget your ultimate goal of contentment in every situation. You can be content with yourself now, but know that you are capable of more. You want to find the bottom-line on where you would be content *and* feel fulfilled. Remember our earlier idea: If you shoot for the sun, but would be very happy on the moon, then we need to define what your "moon" is. These "moons" will be the "Must Haves." If you feel that you now need to add additional goals to your list, hey, that's okay. Add them. It's your list, so do with it as you choose.

For example, if you have written on your list that you want to be the CEO of a Fortune 500 company and make $750,000 a year, but if you would be satisfied to be a top marketing director at the same firm making $150,000 a year, then the latter is what belongs on your "Must Haves" list. And if you would really be satisfied to be an account manager at $50,000 a year, then that's what to put on your "Must Haves" list.

You must always remember your physical and mental attributes as you create your lists. For example, if you know you need an MBA from a top college to become such a CEO, and you currently have an associate degree from a community college, your dream of being the top dog in the company will be contingent on the strength of your educational progress. If being a CEO is your "Must Have" goal, you also need to have the short-term goal of finishing your bachelor's degree and being accepted by a good school for that MBA degree. On the other hand, you need to be realistic. If you dream of playing basketball for the NBA, and you are only 5' 5" tall, your chances for reaching such a goal are very slim. If you do possess the athletic ability to be a professional player, maybe baseball or hockey would be more congruent with your physical attributes.

Break down your 15-year career goals to your basic, realistic "Must Haves." Describe the bottom line of what you would be happy with. However, do not confuse "bottom line" with "settle for." You do not want anything on this list that would be settling for less than you desire and what you are capable of. If you compromise, you will be ultimately unhappy. Your "Must Haves" are what you can live with that would fulfill your life and make you happy.

Spend some time really thinking about your "Must Haves." When you have finished writing, take one of the colored highlighters you have put aside and outline all the Career "Must Haves" on your list. Now we are ready to move on to the "Would Be Nice" list.

The "Would Be Nices" are the next level up from your basic "Must Haves." So, in the case of your career goals, if you decided that you would be happy as a marketing director making $150,000 a year, what would be the next very cool step up? VP of marketing at $350,000? What is the next *attainable* career position and salary level that would be beyond your "Must Haves?" These "Would Be Nices" are higher levels of your goals and, in your mind, must be attainable or within your reach. It may require much effort and determination, but the attainment of it should be a realistic outcome. As before, rework your Extended-Range Career Goals to reflect your "Would Be Nices," and use a different color highlighter to outline them. Now it is time for another quick break for a walk or a snack before we continue.

Once you have had your breather, you are ready to look at "Dream" goals. My favorite! Your dream goals are your ultimate life fantasies. These may or may not be practically attainable, but we always must remember: What one person can do, so can another. Every great, successful person on this planet started out as a helpless baby. What separates the players of life from the watchers is the ability to take action, to follow through, and to have the drive and determination not to settle for second best. Mediocrity is for the unmotivated masses. Excellence comes to those who endeavor to travel a path of success with passion and unwavering faith. Your third highlighter color should be designated for your "Dream" goals.

Now, look over your list once again and outline all of your "Dream" goals. Do not shortchange yourself here. This is the time you shoot for the sun, the stars and, heck, the other galaxies! On this list, you do not work for the company, you own it! Dream big, think outside the lines, be innovative, and dare to dream your biggest dreams. Have fun! Then, when you are finished, put it all down on your list as your "Dream" goals.

Once you have finished with your Extended-Range Career Goals you may choose to stop for this session. Or you may go ahead and repeat the exact same steps for your Extended-Range Family, Personal and Lifestyle Goals. If you decide to finish all of your Extended-Range Goals in one sitting, take a quick break between each area of life and allow a few moments of quiet time to capture the essence of how you visualize your life in 15 years. When you feel ready, set your timer for six minutes and write, write, write!

You may choose to finish all the areas of life of a term in one sitting, or you can break it down into two or more sittings. If you complete one entire term in one sitting, DO NOT move on to another term for at least another day. At a minimum, this entire process will take five days or one day for each term. Do not rush! Rushing the process will only make you tired and frustrated and will not produce the best results. Furthermore, I suggest that you take a day or two between each term to allow the thought and energy of what you have imagined to sink in. You may also want to review and refine your list(s) the day after creating them. I want you to own this process, so do what is comfortable for you, but be careful not to compromise the integrity of the process by hurrying.

Long-Term, Mid-Term, Short-Term Goals

Once you have finished and refined all your Extended-Range Goals, it is time to move on to your Long-Term Goals. Repeat the same processes to create and define these 7-10 year goals just as you did with the 11-15 year Extended-Range Goals. These subsequent goals will be a bit harder to accomplish because we always have to keep in concert with the next greater timeline of the goal list. To create our Long-Term Goals, we have to plan backwards from the Extended-Range Goals lists. Think of your Long-Term Goals as the second-to-the-last step on your ladder of life achievement. Where will you be just prior to attaining all your "Must Haves" at the Extended-Range point?

Think backwards in blocks of years: Where do you see yourself being 7-10 years out, *prior to* achieving all your 11-15 year life goals? This may take some time and thinking, and you may decide to ponder it for a day or two before continuing. This is fine. Every masterpiece takes time, and you are trying to create the masterpiece of your life. So do not rush any part of the goal-setting process. Take as much time as you need to think, create and revise. When you feel ready to tackle the Long-Term Goals, set your timer for six minutes and go for it. Be thorough, and remember the order of the steps.

What we are doing overall is creating some waypoints to chart our progress during our life's journey. Like planning that cross-country trip, we want to know where we will be and have an idea about when we will be there. We are not, at this time, picking all the individual roads we are going to travel, but selecting the main places that we expect to visit along our way and gauging an approximate timeline. Make each subsequent step realistic. It may be extremely difficult to go from being an account manager to CEO, but you can become VP of marketing

Elements of Life Success

easily if you are the current marketing director. Think logically and chronologically. This does not have to be exact. Just estimate what you feel are the steps your life can realistically take. All of these waypoints can be called "Term Goals."

After you have completed your Extended-Range and your Long-Term Goals, move on to the next levels down – to the 4-6 year Mid-Term Goals and the 2-3 year Short-Term Goals. Have all completed goal lists handy as you repeat the process again and again. Remember to think logically and chronologically. At last, you should have only the Immediate Goals left to accomplish. Yet these may be the hardest ones of all to generate.

Immediate Goals

You will find the most effort and the greatest challenges in writing and moving forward with your Immediate Goal Lists. It is from this point on, where you are right now, until the next year or so that will determine all of the future outcomes for you. It will take much of your energy and determination to get the ball rolling, but once in motion the effort will become less as you gain momentum. Now is the time to commit yourself to the task and work your hardest. Remember, the effort you exert now will be comparable to your gains in the future. The greater the effort and commitment, the greater the success! Rome was not built in a day, and nothing great was ever created without action, commitment and tremendous determination. Now is the time that you can control, so take action and commit to following through. The results will be more than worth your early efforts to get the ball rolling.

Now let's tackle those Immediate Goals! What do you have to do right now, today, to start the ball rolling towards your Immediate Goals? What are the tasks you have to accomplish in the next few months to be able to achieve what you want in the next six months to a year? Where do you have to be in a year so that your life will flow toward your next level of wants and desires? When you are ready, set your timer and go for it! Do each life area in turn: Career, Personal, Family and Lifestyle. Remember this process should be easy and fun—use the sheets provided at the end of the chapter in Exercise 10, and refer back to these instructions as much as you have to. When you have finished with the entire process for your Immediate Goals, take a good, long, well-deserved breather.

Congratulations! You have just mapped out your entire life-to-be. As you look at your five stacks of completed goals, congratulate yourself for having the strength to take this first step to the amazing life you deserve to have. Treat yourself to a good dinner or buy yourself something special, because you deserve praise and rewards for the tasks you have just finished. Be proud of yourself and know that you are on your way!

Now that we have created a timeline for the whens and wheres of your life, we can work out a concrete road map of the exact routes you'll need to get through each level of your Term Goals. Next it will be time to make your Action Plan.

-Exercise 10-

Set Your Goals

On the following pages you will find the goal-setting workshop broken down and categorized into terms of years and areas of life for you. Take your time, have fun, and remember that you are about to take control of your life and your destiny.

EXTENDED-RANGE CAREER GOALS
11 to 15 years +

_____

_____

_____

_____

_____

_____

_____

_____

Elements of Life Success

EXTENDED-RANGE FAMILY GOALS
11 to 15 years +

David Michael Ferruolo

EXTENDED-RANGE PERSONAL GOALS
11 to 15 years +

Elements of Life Success

EXTENDED-RANGE LIFESTYLE GOALS
11 to 15 years +

David Michael Ferruolo

LONG-TERM CAREER GOALS
7 to 10 years

Elements of Life Success

LONG-TERM FAMILY GOALS
7 to 10 years

David Michael Ferruolo

LONG-TERM PERSONAL GOALS
7 to 10 years

Elements of Life Success

LONG-TERM LIFESTYLE GOALS
7 to 10 years

MID-TERM CAREER GOALS
4 to 6 years

Elements of Life Success

MID-TERM FAMILY GOALS
4 to 6 years

David Michael Ferruolo

MID-TERM PERSONAL GOALS
4 to 6 years

Elements of Life Success

MID-TERM LIFESTYLE GOALS
4 to 6 years

David Michael Ferruolo

SHORT-TERM CAREER GOALS
2 to 3 years

Elements of Life Success

SHORT-TERM FAMILY GOALS
2 to 3 years

SHORT-TERM PERSONAL GOALS
2 to 3 years

Elements of Life Success

SHORT-TERM LIFESTYLE GOALS
2 to 3 years

David Michael Ferruolo

IMMEDIATE CAREER GOALS
6 months to 1 year

Elements of Life Success

IMMEDIATE FAMILY GOALS
6 months to 1 year

IMMEDIATE PERSONAL GOALS
6 months to 1 year

Elements of Life Success

IMMEDIATE LIFESTYLE GOALS
6 months to 1 year

David Michael Ferruolo

-Chapter 11-

Goals Are Alive!

Like us, goals are living energy. They grow, mature and change as we do. Goals have growth spurts, plateaus, ups and downs and even life spans. We need to be aware of this fact so that we don't get too fixated on the destination and forget to reevaluate our pathway and redirect our progress from time to time. As we mature, our vision of the future typically changes. If we make the decision to change the course of our life, we must also revise our goals.

Unattained and unchanged goals can become massive energy drains that create unnecessary frustration, sadness and even disappointment in your life. You may have lofty goals and a large desires list. If you choose to forego one of your desires, let's say, to get married and start a family, you will necessarily have to reevaluate and revise your goal lists to match your evolving life wants and needs. That earlier plan for marriage and family may turn into a world travel plan instead. Or that once-coveted fancy sports car may just end up being a college fund.

If you leave your dream lists relatively unchanged as your life goes in a different direction, you will have a sense of failure and will no longer feel in control. You must be realistic about your place in life and where it is that you want to go. This does not mean you should throw away your dreams, but rather revise your wants and needs to be more congruent with the new path you have chosen. We must never forget that we make all the choices that dictate our every situation and circumstance. Even when surrounded by unwanted or unpleasant conditions, we have to know that we somehow, somewhere, have made the choices that led us to where we are.

For example, after I graduated from Music Tech College in Minnesota, I wanted to make a living by playing my guitar. I did not care how—in a band, with a studio or for a radio station—anything was okay, as long as I was playing and living. I strived for years to earn enough money to quit my scuba shop job, but I was never able to make a living by just playing guitar.

Finally, I decided to explore a business opportunity back in my hometown in New Hampshire and open my own scuba center. After a bit of research, I decided it was a good move. I could run my own business and also be able to have my guitars there to practice and write songs when I was not busy. I still had a goal of making money by playing guitar.

As time went by, my business grew and my playing diminished, partly because I was focused on making money with the scuba center and partly because there were not many musicians or musical opportunities where I lived. I all but stopped playing. I started getting depressed and frustrated as I looked over my instruments and recording gear gathering dust in the corner of my apartment. I started to think of myself as a failure because my goal of being a full-time musician was unfulfilled. Of course, I felt sour—my life had changed drastically, but my goal had not.

In Minneapolis I'd had the advantage of being in a musical town—one of the best music scenes in the country at the time. There were thousands of other dedicated, professional musicians striving to make a living from their art like me. Every day I met new musical friends, and every day I played for hours with many talented players. I was focused on my goal, and I was in the perfect place to pursue my dreams. New Hampshire, however, was quite different.

It took me about five years to put a band together in New Hampshire. It was hard even to find someone who could or would play, not to mention have the resources, mindset and dedication to make it a full-time gig. I played—for free mostly—for years. In and out of several small bands that only played for fun, I was so saddened by it all that I gave up playing entirely for many years.

When I finally reevaluated my life and my goals, I understood that moving back to New Hampshire was taking me in a new direction and far away from my hope of being a musician full-time. As I began to accept the fact that I was now a businessman and not a professional musician, I was again able to start playing for fun. I had finally redefined my Long-Term Career Goal. So now I play my guitars almost every day in my home and for pleasure. Routinely, I fire up my recording studio and lay down some tracks, but it is for my personal enjoyment and not to cut a record deal. I am much more content with my life and my goals as I periodically manage and adapt them to the road I travel.

So, from time to time, check your vision of where you are and where your want to go. Be diligent in revising and altering your goals to fit your feelings and your life decisions. Remember it is your life to live the way you want to. Do not get too attached to a catalog of material desires. You may just find yourself happy and content without those no-longer-desired items on your long-ago-written lists. Our ultimate goal is contentment, and we may reach that point long before we achieve any of our written goals.

Don't forget that goals are alive—they have a lifespan too. You can become stale and stagnant if you do not refine your goals and create new ones as you achieve and accomplish the old. As your Extended-Range Goals move to your Long-Term Goal list, then Mid-Term, and finally Immediate, you should always be filling the outer categories with new items, so as not to fall into a rut.

This does not mean that when your business is running well, you should quit and start another. And I am definitely not implying that when you get married and have your children, you should just move on if you get bored. I am, however, reminding you to always have emerging dreams and goals—something new to shoot for. If your dream business or job is going well, then maybe it's time to master golf, rock climbing, cooking or guitar playing. Establishing a happy family life is wonderful, but maybe now it's time to write that book, learn to paint or grow that garden. Keeping your body and mind busy is very important to your physical and mental health, and ultimately to living your life happily.

When I was training to become a Navy SEAL, I never thought of the future. My plan was to get my Trident, the symbol of the SEALs, pinned on my uniform. I had no plans or visions of the future beyond the day I became a Frogman! This, of course, caused much suffering in my life.

On that special day, there I stood in front of SEAL Team Two in Little Creek Virginia, and my Trident was about to be pinned to my chest—literally. This ordeal is one of the indoctrinations to being a SEAL. When the 26 weeks of Basic Underwater Demolition/SEAL training are over, and after another year of intense real-life mission training with a SEAL team, you finally qualify for your Trident.

I stood proudly that day, with my platoon lieutenant behind me and the captain of SEAL Team Two in front of me. After a brief speech, the commander held the new, shiny Trident to my chest, and then he punched it as hard as he could, driving the pins into my chest. As the Trident clung to my body and the blood ran down my chest and stomach, the crowd cheered and I was finally a SEAL!

Later, I thought about it: I had lived for that moment for years, but I never thought about what would happen *after* I achieved my dream. Achieving SEAL status was one of the best experiences of my life, but afterwards I felt empty inside. My dream had been fulfilled, and now I had no idea what was I living for. I surfed off that fleeting moment for years, but the dissonance in my soul rose quickly to the surface. Without a new dream, a new direction, something to shoot for, I felt lost and useless. It wasn't until I decided to go to music school that I recaptured the fire inside and felt like I was living again.

Throughout all of my accomplishments, I have always felt down and depressed for a long time after I completed a task. This was partly because I never planned farther out than my one goal and partly because I looked for some kind of inner peace to come from my external accomplishments. Of course, I learned eventually that peace comes from inside and not from external gains.

If we seek our dreams, with our number one goal being peace and happiness, then ultimately, no matter if we reach or fall short of our visions, we will always be content. Remember that contentment comes from inside, from the knowing and loving of yourself, and not from material gain or external success. Unreasonable attachment to your goal list will cause dissonance, for you may mistakenly believe that realizing your goals is the only way to happiness. We know this is not true. Having goals and being happy are separate things entirely. Happiness is a state of mind that can be attained right now, while your goals are something to strive for in your future.

David Michael Ferruolo

-Exercise 11-

Reevaluate Your Goals

Reevaluate the goals you have set. Are there some goals that do not actually serve you any more? Are there some desires that are not congruent with your life as it is today? Which dreams are causing you stress or pain?

List your previous main goals, and then decide whether or not they still serve you. Evaluate each goal and determine whether to modify this goal, cross it off your list, or pursue it with new zest as a life goal.

PAST GOAL 1:

_____

_____

Does this goal still serve me? [ ] YES [ ] NO

Action I should take:
[ ] Modify it [ ] Delete it [ ] Pursue it

PAST GOAL 2:

_____

_____

Does this goal still serve me? [ ] YES [ ] NO

Action I should take:
[ ] Modify it [ ] Delete it [ ] Pursue it

Elements of Life Success

PAST GOAL 3:

_____

_____

Does this goal still serve me? [ ] YES [ ] NO

Action I should take:
[ ] Modify it [ ] Delete it [ ] Pursue it

PAST GOAL 4:

_____

_____

Does this goal still serve me? [ ] YES [ ] NO

Action I should take:
[ ] Modify it [ ] Delete it [ ] Pursue it

PAST GOAL 5:

_____

_____

Does this goal still serve me? [ ] YES [ ] NO

Action I should take:
[ ] Modify it [ ] Delete it [ ] Pursue it

-Chapter 12-

Take Action: Motion Is Progress

Think of your life as a five-story building with each floor representing your five levels of Term Goals. You are located in the basement, and the Immediate Goals are the first floor of the building. It would be nice if there were an express elevator right to the top, but in this particular building there are only five flights of stairs.

Each individual stair on a flight represents an Action Step, and each Action Step or stair has to be taken, in order for you to make it up the next level or flight of stairs. Because we can only take action to get where we are going from where we currently are, we must concentrate our thought and effort on the things we have to do *now*. An Action Plan focuses us on the tasks at hand to propel us toward the next level of our building, and it keeps us on track as we rise to the top.

What is the first thing that you must do to get the ball rolling toward your Immediate Goals? Sometimes this is a hard question, but if we take an inventory of where we are right now and then compare it to our listed Immediate Goals, the steps become clearer. So where are you right now? The same process you used to create your goals can now help you to determine your current place in life. For this process, you will need a pen or pencil, four different colored highlighter pens, and a stapler. Remember to use the exercise worksheets provided for you at the end of this chapter as a guide.

On the first page of Exercise 12, labeled "My Current Career Situation," grab your pen or pencil and get ready to work. Without thinking and without bias or judgment, describe your current job situation using the same method we used earlier, in Chapter 9, to define our goals.

Be objective—try writing your job description as if it were about someone else. If it helps you, imagine that a friend has asked you to help him or her with this project, and you are the transcriber. But be truthful—this process is about you and for you. The more honest you are with yourself about your current career situation, the more powerful the change will be as you move forward. Once you have completed your Current Career Situation, you can then compare it with your Immediate Career Goals, and finally begin to create your Career Action Steps.

What are your first few important steps? That is the question to ask yourself as you compare your Current Situation with your Immediate Goals list. As you look over these two pages side by side, list as many action steps as you can see necessary to accomplish your 6-months to 1-year Career Goals. At this point, do not think chronologically or logically, just list the things you have to do. Try to be as thorough as possible, listing out as many detailed action steps as you can, and using the provided worksheets plus any extra pieces of paper you may need.

Once you have completed the detailed list of all the Action Steps needed to reach your Immediate Career Goal, then you need to prioritize them. For this, you will need four colored highlighters to separate your list into four parts:

A-list (first color): These steps are basic and mandatory for creating your "Must Have" life. They are the first action steps you have to take in order to build the foundation for everything else to come. These are the things you have to do immediately. Without doing these things first, you will have a very hard time completing anything else.

B-list (second color): These are the highly important, but not mandatory steps, which will reinforce attaining your "Must Haves" and help to elevate your life towards the "Would Be Nice" category.

C-list (third color): The steps in this category become mandatory only if you wish to attain your "Would Be Nice" goals. These steps are loftier and will require more energy and motivation. To achieve the C-list, you will have to be unusually determined and focused.

D-list (fourth color): This is your "Dream Goal" category. These are the steps necessary to create the life of your dreams. Attempting these tasks will take a tremendous amount of commitment, enthusiasm and perseverance. These tasks will require much personal sacrifice from you, but they will pay you back with the most amazing outcomes.

When you have broken down your Action Steps into your A, B, C and D lists, you will know exactly what to do right now to start your life transformation in this area. Review your lists and put a star next to all the most important tasks you have to accomplish right away or within the next one to three weeks. Once you have identified the most immediate and important steps, then start numbering them. Whatever you designate as "Number One" is the step that you feel is most pressing. Pick out the top three items on your list and commit yourself to taking action on them starting now. Even if you do not know quite what to do, take *some* action now, even if it's just reading or research. Motion is progress, so move forward. Make a commitment to yourself to do something on your list every day.

When you have finished with your Career Action Steps, then it will be time to go through the same process in each of the other areas – Family, Personal, and Lifestyle – in order to create a complete Action Plan for your life. Again, use the rest of the exercise sheets at the end of this chapter. Be sure to take breaks as necessary between each area. Do not spend more than 15 minutes on each page of the exercise—your first thoughts are usually your best ones.

Sometimes it is hard to know which steps to take in the beginning. Some people can look at their Action Steps lists and simultaneously act on many fronts. However, other people must proceed in a more linear manner. It is just as effective to pick out the most important thing you have to do first and to start there. Also, some things cannot be done until others are finished. There will be a chronological order that is natural to your steps.

You now have a detailed road map of exactly where you want to go and exactly how to get there. It is solely up to you to keep the ball rolling. Remember, your Action Plan is as alive as you and your goals are. It will require constant upkeep and revision. Look at your Action Plan daily and make sure that you are still on the right path. You may need to revise, add, subtract or sometimes completely re-think your Action Plan to suit the ever-changing world and the ever-evolving you. But this is your path, and you are in total control. You can choose to change or redirect the course of your life whenever you choose. Just make sure that you keep your "Must Haves" at the front of your mind.

You will, as we all do, encounter some snags and pitfalls along the way, but as you do, just remember that this is your life and you can choose how to live it. Keep your thoughts positive. Affirm daily that you are on the right path, and know that you can make it happen. Now that you have well-defined Goals and a solid Action Plan, take action! Use your power and don't look back!

-Exercise 12-

Creating Your Action Plan

Begin your personal Action Plan here, using the instructions from the opening pages of Chapter 12. Be honest with yourself, be specific in your descriptions, and get ready to take charge of your destiny!

MY CURRENT CAREER SITUATION

CAREER SITUATION ACTION STEPS

Elements of Life Success

MY CURRENT FAMILY SITUATION

David Michael Ferruolo

FAMILY SITUATION ACTION STEPS

Elements of Life Success

MY CURRENT PERSONAL SITUATION

David Michael Ferruolo

PERSONAL SITUATION ACTION STEPS

Elements of Life Success

MY CURRENT LIFESTYLE SITUATION

David Michael Ferruolo

LIFESTYLE SITUATION ACTION STEPS

Elements of Life Success

David Michael Ferruolo

-Chapter 13-

Confronting Your Fears

"What are you afraid of?' I asked. "I don't know," my friend replied. "Then just go ask," I said. "No way. I can't. I just can't." My friend was driving me crazy. As we sat in the restaurant nibbling on nachos, I tried to figure out what was so hard about getting someone to ask a simple question. You see, my friend was pining for our very attractive, single waitress. We knew she was single because finally I asked her. During casual conversation, we found out that she liked to do many of the things my friend liked to do. I also knew, by the way she smiled at him, that she was interested too.

"Please," I said, "just go ask for her number. I'm sure she'll give it to you." He just shook his head with a defeatist look on his face. Baffled, I asked, "What's the worst that can happen? She will say no. And then you will know and not be so frustrated thinking about her all the time." "No," he said adamantly. I tried to get to the root of his trepidations, but to no avail. Every time I asked why he would not ask her out, he just said, "I can't." Well, I thought, I'm not working tonight, so I changed the subject and we ordered more food. Fear is such an amazing thing, I thought, as I wolfed down my southwest chicken salad.

So what is fear anyway? In my humble opinion, most fears are hypothetical worries about uncertain events or happenings in the future. It's as simple as that. We are afraid of something that has not yet happened. We create a situation about what we think may happen to us, and we become fearful of the hypothetical outcome. Is it logical to fear what does not yet exist?

Fear is the psychological, emotional and physiological response to our thoughts about a present or future situation. Fear evokes our most basic responses: fight or flight. Some fears are very healthy, of course, when your safety or well-being are obviously at risk. But even these healthy fears are sometimes illogical! Fear can lead to panic, and panic can cloud your mind and paralyze you. Ironically, it is this fear/panic reaction, and not the actual situation itself, that is the downfall of most people.

It was mid-winter one year when I was called to help out with a snowmobile accident. The driver had hit a pressure ridge—a place where two mammoth sheets of ice come together forming a ridge that sometimes creates a gap. It was in one of these gaps that the snowmobile had fallen through. The driver had survived the accident and had called my company to recover the snowmobile. I brought my crew to the site and suited up in my ice-diving equipment. One of my senior instructors was my diving buddy that day.

When we were satisfied that all the safety lines were in place, we plunged into the icy depths, some 60 feet below a three-foot-thick ceiling of ice. As we descended, it grew darker and darker. I flicked on my diving light, and with my buddy nearby, we started our search pattern. The visibility was very poor, and I could barely make out my dive buddy's silhouette only a few feet away. The contour of the lake's bottom was so black, it seemed to have no end. Occasionally, I would put my hand out in front of me to feel the bottom. My dive light would disappear into the silt and a bloom of dark bottom matter would engulf me. Although in the frigid cold, my heart was beating rapidly and I was trickling with sweat inside my diving mask.

After a several minutes, I noticed my buddy's erratic breathing pattern. He was staying a few feet above me, and his eyes were fixated on my bright yellow air tank. I held my hand up in the okay sign, and he responded positively. Although I could see the apprehension in his gaze, we continued the search. About 15 minutes into the dive, my diving partner frantically tugged on the buddy line and gave me the "up" signal. I waved him a goodbye, and he slowly ascended. I reluctantly continued on alone.

After about an hour, my air cylinder was low, so I returned to the safety of the icy surface, relieved to be out of the cold and darkness. As I rose to the surface, I could see that my dive buddy was sitting nearby, shaking his head and smiling. I smiled back and took off my mask, and before I could speak, he said; "The boogie man was down there. I was scared shitless," and we both laughed.

Later that day we talked about what had happened. Although he was a very experienced diver, he said he kept thinking about all the things that could go wrong 60 feet under the ice in 32-degree, pitch-black waters with only one small hole for escape, and he could not keep his panic at bay. His vast experience could not comfort him, and his anxiety forced him to abort the dive. There was no real peril. I dived for another 45 minutes after his retreat without incident—and alone!

What do we actually fear in those stressful situations? Think about that question for a moment. In such a predicament, what are we really afraid of? Is it the present threats? Is it the possible outcomes? Or is it the unknown? My dive buddy was in no harm or any imminent danger, yet he panicked—why?

Fear of the unknown is so ingrained in our minds and influenced by the books we read, the movies we watch and the stories we hear from our parents, friends and teachers. Fear is so much more likely to be hypothetical than factual. If we think about it, social conditioning is the root of most of our daily fears. We are not really sure how something will turn out, so we search our minds for the information we have stored from the stories of others' lives.

For instance, I met a young girl on a plane who was petrified of flying. I asked her how many times she had flown, and she replied that this was her second time. I asked her what happened on her first flight to make her dislike flying so much. She said nothing happened, and that she had slept the whole time. So I asked why she was so afraid?

Well, her grandfather had died in a small plane crash when she was about three years old. She does not remember him or anything about the accident, but her family talks about the crash often. They bring it up at family events, and everyone talks about how dangerous flying is. This poor 13-year-old girl has been told, in effect programmed to believe, that flying is dangerous. For 10 years she has been bombarded with these beliefs from others, and now she is petrified of flying. I gave her a lot of credit for getting on a plane the second time. She, of course, slept the entire flight.

What are you afraid of right now? Is it the fear of success, of failure, of not being good enough, of what others will think of you? What are your current fears? Whether your phobia is an aversion to spiders, heights, deep water, dark places or flying, that fear, in my opinion, is always in truth the same—the fear of the unknown.

And yet, the uncertainty of the future is the spice of life. It is what actually gives us the power to create our opportunities. Nothing is certain and nothing is written in stone, so our decisions and actions can dictate how the future will unfold. Having well-defined goals, a comprehensive action plan and the ability to execute your decisions will dictate your future. Giving in to self-generated fears will only keep you in a place of dissonance and block you from getting those sought-after "Must Haves" in your life. Changing your fear-based thinking into feelings of empowerment and self-confidence will positively affect your ability to control and create your own destiny. Know that most fears are only illusionary—they are created by thought. You have the ability to direct you own thought.

Elements of Life Success

Choosing to face the uncertainty of the future head-on, with enthusiasm and vigor, will propel you past your fears.

Instead, choose to welcome your fears, to confront them directly and to give them names, colors and tastes. When you let yourself become familiar with what holds you back, you can easily move beyond your doubts and embrace the future. Do you think you might be better off if you had foreknowledge of the events of your life? You would then know everything that was going to transpire. Every second of every day would be known to you, and no matter what you did to alter the future, you would already know the outcome. Where would be the adventure, mystery, and fun? What would be the sense of living if we knew what was going to happen? At this moment, you feel alive *because of* all the uncertainty and choices life holds.

There is great power in knowing that you can choose what happens in your life. Right now, you have the ability to choose your every action and reaction. You are in control of your existence at this very moment. Do not concern yourself over the non-existent future. Know that you are molding it right now.

Identifying Your Fears

To change your thoughts from fear to optimism and power, you must first know what you are fearful of. For this process, you will need to refer to your Immediate Goals lists. You will again use the worksheets at the end of this chapter and need a pen or pencil, two different colored highlighters and all of your term goal lists.

Start with your Career Fears list first. Have all of your Term Goal lists bookmarked for quick review, and turn them each to the Career pages. Now, as you scan over the Career Goal lists, identify and write down as many fears as you can think of that are blocking you from attaining these goals. Set your timer for 15 minutes and keep writing until the timer goes off. Once you have finished with your "Career Fears," take a short break, and then move on to your "Family Fears," "Personal Fears," and "Lifestyle Fears." Each time, remember to set your timer for 15 minutes, and do not stop until the timer goes off. Please remember to take a short breather between each phase of the process.

Now that you have identified all of the fears associated with living a truly amazing and successful life, what do you do with them? I say just crumple them up and toss them in the trash! Could it be just that easy? Why not? As foolish as this may seem as a solution, it is no more irrational than the fears themselves. My solution and your problem both have no true logical basis to them. If it is illogical to fear what does not exist, then why should we apply logic, thought or a complex process to solve the problem? To me, this is a waste of energy. And throwing your "Fear" papers into the wastebasket can serve as a powerful symbol of your control over your own illusions. And yet I know that sometimes the mind has to replace what is gone with a new train of thought.

Transforming Fear into Empowerment

If you decide that simply throwing away your list of fears will not work for you, let's try a very effective process that I have used successfully to move past my own fears. Look over your fear lists and find the most common fearful traits that are in each list. In using this technique with many others and myself, I have noticed that all the fears and doubts on all the pages are similar—they can usually be narrowed down to several core worries.

Not Succeeding: Those who simply fear failing and not being able to do what they set out to accomplish.

Not Being Good Enough: Those who fear that they will be not necessarily a failure but somehow inadequate and not up to standard.

Not Being Accepted: Those who are afraid of being rejected. They fear that family, friends and society will discard their ideas, dreams and aspiration as not worthwhile or, worse yet, that they will be unloved or discarded.

Being Embarrassed: Those who are afraid of looking silly or being humiliated. Despite accomplishing their tasks, some people fear that they will look bad while doing it.

Feeling Guilt: Those who feel, or are made to feel, guilty about the nay-sayers or the unmotivated individuals that they may be leaving behind.

Feeling Isolated: Those who fear being alone with no support as they venture out of their comfort zone and their familiar circle of friends.

David Michael Ferruolo

When we can place all of our fears into such identifiable categories, we can then begin to redirect our mindset toward more positive thoughts of encouragement, empowerment and support. Let's see if we can take the above six fears and change the way we think about them:

Transform "Not Succeeding" into "I Am Doing My Best": It's not whether you actually succeed, but the character and quality you show in the pursuit that forms your life. Many great men and women in history failed many times before becoming successful. What others will remember about you is not the grandiosity of your achievements, but rather how you lived with honor, character and passion. These values are the most successful things you can possess. Even what you may consider *not* succeeding *is* succeeding if it is viewed as one more point on the continuum of success. Remember, when things don't work out the way we think they should, we learn important lessons that will make us more successful in the long run.

Transform "Not Being Good Enough" into "At Least I'm Doing Something": There are so many people not doing what they want to do. Those who have the courage and choose to follow their dreams should be proud they have taken action—any action—toward making their dreams a reality. It is not to be *the* best but rather to be *your* best that makes you successful. Successful people always have many critics. I say, "Bring 'em on." The more critics I have, the more attention I am getting and the more successful I am becoming. Relish the thought that you are a winner, an achiever, and that you have the power to create your life.

Transform "Not Being Accepted" into "I Am Unique and Creative": I have found that the only difference between being labeled strange and therefore unacceptable, and being labeled eccentric and therefore desirable by many, is whether or not you have succeeded according to others' standards. Don't blame yourself or your ideas and dreams for your family's, friends' or society's lack of understanding of your passion to succeed. Know that the only acceptance you really need is from yourself. If you believe in your destiny, what does it matter if few others see your vision? Your acceptance of yourself and your path is all you need.

Transform "Being Embarrassed" into "Always Laugh at Yourself First": How can you possibly feel humiliated if you are fun-loving and humorous about yourself all the time? Laugh at yourself! Laugh with others at what you do! If it warrants laughter, laugh! You can't be humiliated if you can see and embrace the irony of the situation. If you keep your ego in check and humbly, passionately, pursue your dreams, what embarrassment can come from that? Laugh at yourself, say "Oops," and pick up the pieces as you move forward. Know that this too will pass, and realize that you were brave enough to take the chance when many others could not or did not. Accept the situation for what it is – a passing moment on the way to your dreams.

Transform "Feeling Guilty" into "I'm Deserving of All That Comes My Way": Philanthropy was born from those who have achieved great monetary abundance and decided to give back to the world. Know that as you become more successful and gain abundance, you too have a choice to give back and help those around you. Do not feel guilty about your accomplishments, but embrace the good that comes from your heart. Who is more deserving than one who works with passion from a place of truth and integrity? The anger that others less fortunate than yourself send you is only a misdirected form of pity for themselves. When others are jealous and envious, they will try to make you feel guilty about the things you have – not because you have them, but because they do not. Do not accept this "gift" of guilt, and then you will be free of its burdens.

Transform "Feeling Isolated" into "In Transition to a Newer, Better Place": It is true that when you endeavor to follow your dreams, your family and friends may become your worst critics. Sometimes these "Dream Killers," as I call them, are just those who are negative out of spite and jealousy. Sometimes, however, they are trying to protect and shelter you. Those who never did and never will go after their dreams may not be able to see clearly through the blinders of their own world. It is from a place of ignorance that they react to your vision. Pity them and leave them behind as you move on. As you move up the ladder of life success, you will meet many wonderful and like-minded people who will share your motivation, zeal and ideas. It is not lonely at the top, only on the elevator ride up.

Using this process of recasting the negative into the positive will work for any and all of the fears you have. It will free you to create the life you desire and deserve. Identify the fear, recognize its negative side, and simply find its positive side. The things you look at will seem different if you change the way you perceive them. Work actively to change your thoughts of fear and negativity to ones of optimism and success, and then watch your life blossom!

-Exercise 13-

Transforming Your Fears

Use the process of recasting the negative into the positive to change your feelings about the fears you have. Identify the fear, recognize its negative side, and simply find its positive side. Write how it feels to change your thoughts of fear and negativity to ones of optimism and success.

MY CURRENT CAREER FEARS

Elements of Life Success

TURN MY CAREER FEARS INTO EMPOWERMENT

David Michael Ferruolo

MY CURRENT FAMILY FEARS

Elements of Life Success

TURN MY FAMILY FEARS INTO EMPOWERMENT

MY CURRENT PERSONAL FEARS

Elements of Life Success

TURN MY PERSONAL FEARS INTO EMPOWERMENT

MY CURRENT LIFESTYLE FEARS

Elements of Life Success

TURN MY LIFESTYLE FEARS INTO EMPOWERMENT

David Michael Ferruolo

-Chapter 14-

Overcoming Your Obstacles

Every competitive person living life with passion and zeal loves a challenge, so consider every obstacle an opportunity to shine. Every time people encounter a hardship along the road to success, they either fall below it or rise above it. Trudging ahead with dedication and determination is what forges our character. In such times of adversity, we and the others around us learn who we are and what we are made of.

It is not those quiet moments of solitude and ease that show what we are capable of, but rather facing the storm head-on that brings out our best. James Allen wrote in his classic work, *As a Man Thinketh*: "Circumstance does not make the man; it reveals him to himself." We never really know what we are made of until we have faced challenge and adversity.

Look back upon your life and think of a time when you encountered and overcame obstacles and hardship. Remember that feeling of elation, accomplishment and pride as you persevered? There is nothing quite like the feeling of achieving despite adversity. Obstacles need not be avoided. They offer us the chance to shine and grow—to see what we are made of. I have come to welcome challenge, and through my life's many obstacles, I have been able to identify the five phases of overcoming adversity. I found that when I broke down tough situations into their parts, they were much easier to deal with.

1. The Overwhelming Chore: When an obstacle is staring us in the face, it sometimes seems like an overwhelming or impossible task to overcome. Frustration and helplessness are common feelings when your dreams seem to have come to a halt. This is not the time to quit, however, but the time to take action.

2. The Decision: First, you must make the decision: Give up, find another direction or go for it. If you analyze your situation with a clear mind and all your intelligence, you will find solutions. And when you make the decision to move forward into uncertainty or into adversity, you will truly be forging your own destiny.

3. The Resolve: Even when you have made the initial decision, there will be a point where you will want to quit. It happens to everybody. Keep in mind that there is a positive solution to every situation, and stand your ground with strength and determination. Sometimes the answer to your challenge may be unclear or the solution elusive, but trust me, it is there. Keep a positive outlook. Search for the best way over, around, under or through the roadblock. It will feel good to hang in there, no matter what happens—you will feel alive.

4. The Other Side: Finally comes the time that you will see light at the end of the tunnel. At this point, remember your feelings of elation and accomplishment from surpassing the previous obstacles. Now, let the feeling that you could do anything sweep through you. You are on fire, and nothing can stop you now.

5. The Lessons Learned: Once through to the other side, look back and see all the things you overcame. Let yourself feel good about yourself, knowing you have what it takes to forge ahead despite all the obstacles. Simultaneously, be humble and see the lessons and the messages this path had for you. The greatest learning and the best personal growth take place when adversity forces us to gain understanding and knowledge about ourselves.

Obstacles are like modern-day rites-of-passage. In tribal times, for example, men had to prove themselves worthy of being warriors by overcoming difficult challenges. Whether living alone in the wilderness for an extended time, or facing a wild predatory animal one-on-one, or climbing the highest mountain and living there with no food or water for days, the boy who could meet these challenges was considered to have become a man.

Were these tests for the benefit of the tribe or the person who faced the challenge? Well, I believe the elders knew that every boy eventually becomes a man and turns into an able warrior, but the boy does not know what he is capable of until he is tested. It is during these tests that he develops self-awareness, confidence and esteem. There is a big difference between *thinking* you can and *knowing* you can. How do you know what you are capable of unless you are tested?

    Today's world is not without its testing venues. The military, college and the workplace are good examples of testing grounds. Boot camp allows men and women to know what they are made of, so that they can perform in the face of battle. Academia challenges students to learn, create and produce under the pressure of exams and time, so they can survive within their careers. Certain jobs present workers with situations that challenge their abilities daily to perform their duties optimally.

    Military service and Ivy League colleges do produce some of the most well-rounded and capable people in the world. But for the general populace, the School of Life is the greatest teacher and preparer of proficient people. So welcome your obstacles as challenges, and face them head-on with creativity, determination and a clear mind. Learn the lessons from each hardship in life that will allow you to develop, mature and grow. Here are some tried-and-true methods for dealing with life's daily tests.

10 Steps for Moving Past Obstacles

1. Clear Your Mind.

When faced with any challenge, the first thing you must do is to think through all aspects of the problem thoroughly. Sometimes, getting away from the situation will give you some time to breathe, relax and think with a clearer head. When I'm facing a hurdle, I often take a long lunch or leave a bit early to go hiking or kayaking, but you should do whatever works for you. When the mind is relaxed, it can think much more clearly and intelligently. Also, when the body is involved in subtly repetitious actions like walking, biking, running, swimming or kayaking, the mind tends to wander in a positive way. In this relaxed thinking state, the mind is more creative, more productive and more able to see outside of the box with clearer vision.

2. Define Your Goals.

Once you have spent some quality time pondering the possibilities in a particular challenge, you need to realign yourself with your goals. Reconnecting with why you are on this path will enhance your power and will help you to see it through. If you want it badly, and if you know you can do it, you are already half-way home to achieving any goal. This is a great time to review your goal lists and make sure your passion is on a true course. If you feel the need to adjust or change your goals, do so.

Sometimes, as we travel a path, we find out that it really is not for us after all. Some doors will open when we are living with passion and awareness, and some will close.

Make sure that you choose wisely which doors to walk through. If you are on track with your goals, and if you have reaffirmed your driving desire to overcome what is in your way, then the next steps will greatly help you to overcome any obstacles.

3. Break It Down into Parts.

Obstacles can seem mammoth when looking at the whole, but sometimes the smaller parts of a single obstacle have smaller solutions. A wall may seem impossible and impregnable, but on closer inspection it may reveal cracks, holes and weak spots that can be easily exploited. What are the areas of your current problem that can be taken care of easily? What are the smaller parts of the whole? Using the exercise sheets at the end of this chapter, describe:

"My Current Obstacle"

Randomly on the page, anywhere you choose to, write down as many smaller parts of the big obstacle—your wall—that you can possibly think of. Get creative and think beyond the obvious. There are many facets to every situation, so concentrate and be thorough. When you are finished, mark off all the parts by drawing lines around each component. You have now sectioned down your wall into manageable parts! And any wall can come down, no matter how big. You just have to start chipping away, and with good intentions and determination, eventually it will fall.

A few years ago, I bought my first home. It was a "fixer-upper," and I did not have the know-how or the talents to tackle many of the projects. The obstacle was that

I needed to move in within two weeks, and the home was not ready to house my family. Every part of every room needed something. I was overwhelmed and on the verge of a breakdown. A friend suggested I create a list. A good suggestion, really, but it only added to my stress when I began looking at two pages of pending projects. Frustrated, I ripped up the list and threw it on the floor. As I stared at the small pieces of paper on the floor, I had an epiphany.

I could see two simple projects clearly, within this pile of ripped paper: First, pull up the living room carpet, and second, paint the spare bedroom. Well, I can do *that*, I thought. I grabbed my tools and was finished with both projects in a few hours. Then I made a new list—in a completely new way.

This time I ripped up a blank sheet of paper first, and I wrote a part of the project on each piece. There were a lot of pieces, so I then divided the pieces into four categories: Immediate "I Can Dos" and Immediate "I Need Helps." These two categories definitely needed to get done before we could move in. I then created two more categories of tasks that could be done later, while we were living in the house. They were: Leisurely "I Can Dos" and Leisurely "I Need Helps."

So now I knew which projects I could get done at once, which ones I could tackle myself later, and which ones would require assistance. One of the immediate things to do was find some help, and of course, after a few calls to friends, with promises of all-you-can-eat pizza, I had all the help I needed. I finished the tasks and moved in with one day to spare. Naturally, I'm still working on the other tasks.

4. Consider All the Options.

Analyze the state of affairs from all angles and directions. Remove yourself from the situation and get a bird's eye view of it. Remember, the obstacle only blocks your current viewpoint, so any small adjustment may alleviate the circumstance. Take on a broad perspective—a multi-dimensional view. Looking at the roadblocks with linear vision will not let you see other possible paths. Write down all possible avenues, passageways and outlets, over, around, under or through whatever stands in your way. Most of the time, solutions are simple if you change your perspective. As a guide, use the worksheet at the end of this chapter headed:

"My Options"

Take time to consider: What are the different perspectives on your problem? What avenues offer ways around, over, under or through your problem? You have broken down your problem into smaller parts. Now list as many possible solutions as you can think of for each piece of the puzzle. Feel free to use as many more pieces of paper as you need.

No matter how mainstream or how far-fetched your ideas might sound, write them down. Think from all angles and perspectives. Make it a game: How many solutions can you find to this piece of the challenge? Can you find five, ten, twenty, fifty? Do this process for all the parts of your problem. Once you have listed all your options for all the parts on the provided worksheets, you can begin to analyze the multitude of solutions, choose the best ones, and create a specialized action plan to conquer each part of the obstacle.

5. Make an Obstacle Action Plan

You should now have considered all the options and broken down your problem into many different parts. Guess what—your hardest work is already done! All you have to do now is prioritize the solutions in order of their importance and their natural timeline.

Look at the "My Options" sheet for your challenge's first part, and figure out which one is the most important and which one needs to be done first. You may only have a few sheets, or you may have ended up with multitudes. The number doesn't matter—just put them in order of their importance. Once you have them in order, staple them together and number the pages. When that is done, get out your calendar or day planner, and set a deadline by when you will have each part of the problem solved.

I know that many of us hate to write things down. Sometimes we tell ourselves that it is a pain, or slows our thinking, or is too much like homework. But it is important to crystallize our thoughts by writing them down. That is the only way we can make our goals real, and make ourselves accountable for achieving what we really want.

Remember, like goals, problems are alive and can change with time, so know that constant revision and analysis will be required. When you have decided on your timeline, write the completion date for each piece on the corresponding sheet of paper and highlight it with a yellow highlighter. Congratulations, you now have a solid order and a timeline for surpassing part one of your obstacle! At this point, I'll bet your huge obstacle seems more like a minor nuisance. Attacking your problem head-on in this manner will minimize its power over you. When you see the options available and know that you will soon move through them, your "obstacle" becomes just a series of tasks.

For each part of your problem, then, you should have many possible solutions. You must now prioritize each set of options in order of workability and success. Do this by using the worksheets at the end of this chapter called:

"My Obstacle Action Plan"

Go through each list and number it. Place the best solution first and so forth. Sometimes several options should be considered at the same time, so you could give the same number to several options if you want them to have the same priority. By the time you have done this exercise for each part, your road map to success will be complete.

You should now have a detailed Obstacle Action Plan, a decisive road map to the other side of your problem. Now all you have to do is commit to it and take action!

6. Look at It from the Other Side.

Before I start, I always like to take a few moments to visualize what my world will look and feel like once I have overcome this adversity. I suggest you try this simple technique. It is very powerful and will give you confidence to take the necessary actions to follow through.

Close your eyes and propel yourself into the future. Try to see yourself as if you were several years *beyond* your major obstacle. See that your life is amazing and feel that all the hard work and perseverance has paid off. Feel in your gut the essence of your newly created world. You are elated and are now able to reap the benefits of all your determination and hard work. One by one, your problems have been solved, and you are where you want to be. There is no more weight on your shoulders, no stress, no pain; only harmony, peace and abundance remain.

Look back at the road that you traveled to get to this point, and see in retrospect how worth the trip it really was. Know that it was only your perceptions—the illusions in your mind—that created your stresses and pitfalls. You know now there are no permanent obstacles, only challenges with many solutions. Your life is so good, so blessed, and you are so glad that you took the time and made the effort to get to where you now are. This very small amount of time and sweat were well worth it to enjoy the rest of your life.

7. Keep Using Positive Thinking.

Does all this sound too easy? It might, especially if the task of Life Success seems overwhelming and you are a little apprehensive about the process. The power of positive thinking will greatly help you to see the way. Keep your thoughts focused only on what you do want. Avoid thinking about what you don't want. Try to visualize the end result, and you will actually be able to see yourself breaking through to the other side. Train your mind to be looking for the positive possibilities. You can *learn* to see the glass as half full, not half empty.

The way you think and talk will have a direct effect on your actual situation, so keep your thinking and your speaking positive. Try to redirect your mindset toward a more passive tone by using less harsh words to describe your situation. Remember the words of Dr. Wayne Dyer in his book, *Power of Intention:* "If you change the way you look at things, the things you look at change." If you stay positive, you can gain the power to re-create your life.

My Old Words	*My New Words*
Obstacle	Challenge
Road Block	Opportunity
Wall	Minor Delay
Barrier	Hindrance
Dead End	Postponement
Stalemate	In Process

8. Commit Yourself to the Task.

On all levels, it is now time to commit to solving your problem—mentally, emotionally and physically. Affirm to yourself that there *is* a solution and that you *will* find it. Know that you already have the ability and the fortitude to see it through to the end, and you will not quit. Make a pact with yourself that you will do everything and anything to dissolve the problems in your way. You are now a soldier going into battle. You are proud and honorable, with integrity and fortitude. Know that you will prevail. Know that it is worth it. Commit—and go for it.

9. Don't Beat Your Head Against the Wall.

There is a reason that we do so much thinking and planning before we start breaking down the walls of our obstacle. Sometimes our solutions just will not work. When you've come to the end of the path, and you know that an option is truly exhausted, do not keep trying and do not keep beating your head against the wall. Fail fast! By fail fast, I mean know when something is not going to work and move on immediately. Don't give up prematurely, out of frustration or laziness, but know when to shift your energy to another possible solution on you list.

The work you do will not be futile. In most cases, the "dead end" occurs because some work on another part of the problem must be done before you can move farther along your current path. You have your detailed Obstacle Action Plan to guide you through, so when you hit a so-called dead end, either move on to another solution or create another plan to get through where you are. Know that not all solutions are going to work. Sometimes it will be very frustrating, and you'll think the cause is lost, but don't give up. Fail fast, regroup, look over your Action Plan and move on. There is a solution to every problem—it may be unclear right now, but it is there. If you keep trying with a resolute mind and intelligent thought, you will find the way.

10. Pat Yourself on the Back.

I see so many people being negative after they have come through a major roadblock, and I do not understand why. For example, some say things like, *"Was it worth it?"* Or, when I try to congratulate them on a job well done, they come up with a million "*buts*" to minimize their glory. This kind of thinking drains your energy. Allow yourself to savor the feeling of accomplishment, and congratulate yourself. Stand tall in the power of knowing that you are able to move through obstacles – that you, and nothing and nobody else, are in charge of your destiny. Give yourself a pat on the back. Do not lose momentum, but use your newfound accomplishments to boost your commitment to your dreams.

-Exercise 14-

Overcoming Obstacles

In the space below, at random intervals, write or sketch all the smaller parts of your big obstacle—your wall—that you can possibly think of. In other words, make a visual map of the problem. Get creative and think beyond the obvious. There are many facets to every situation, so concentrate and be thorough. When you are finished, mark off the parts by drawing lines around each component. This will help you section your wall into manageable parts.

My Current Obstacle

My Options

Now create as many options as you can for dealing with each part:

My Obstacle Action Plan

Finally, write a plan using all the parts of your problem and all your options for overcoming each part and the whole:

Elements of Life Success

David Michael Ferruolo

-Chapter 15-

Feel Your Way Through

This world has so very much to offer that the choices are sometimes overwhelming. There are so many interesting careers, places to live and things to do. With all these choices, how do we know which ones are right for us? I believe that inside all of us we have the ability to truly know what we want. We have an internal guidance system that continually alerts us and makes us aware of whether or not a decision is congruent with our inner wants and needs. Our emotions are the inner gauge as to what is good or not good for us in our lives.

We all have had those gut feelings and lingering sensations that urge us to do or not do something. I've heard so many stories that begin with the words, "I knew I should have gone ahead, but I didn't trust my gut." When a situation goes awry, I also have often heard, "Oh, I just knew I shouldn't have done that. I had a bad feeling, but I did it anyway." Learning to hear your emotional voice—or your spirit as some call it—is very important. And listening to it is imperative if you wish to achieve your dreams. This over-stimulating world in which we live can make it difficult to hear that quiet voice of the spirit and therefore not easy to discern what we really want and like. We all have a massive range of emotions that constantly talk to us throughout our days and nights. Getting in touch with your inner voice will dramatically help you see more clearly and make better choices for your life.

When faced with a decision, first ask yourself the question: "How do I really feel about that?" Take a moment and relax. What are your instincts telling you? What emotions are prevalent as you think of the situation? Are you getting good or bad vibrations? Trusting your inner vibes is a powerful way to steer clear of unwanted circumstances and bring you closer to what you truly need in your life. Emotions are at work whenever you are thinking. If you stop and become aware of them, they offer you a constant signaling process—either positive or negative—that can help you to make up your mind. Positive emotions mean "Go ahead," and negative ones mean "Steer clear."

And what about all those times we were taught *not* to trust and honor our emotions over logic or reason? Emotions are often said to be "misleading," "selfish," "needy, or "childish." Yes, following our emotions from a place of fear and insecurity will mostly always lead to unfulfilling situations. However, trusting our inner voice from a place of surrender and personal power—while releasing fear, negativity and insecurity—will allow us to make better, clearer decisions for now and for the future.

Below is a list of positive and negative emotional signals. Look over the list and see how easy it would be to redirect the way you are thinking so that you may hear your inner voice clearly and perceive your world a bit differently. Labeling can be very empowering, if you choose to hear and to use the right words.

Positive Emotional Signals	Negative Emotional Signals
Animated	Angry
Anticipating	Anxious
Aroused	Apathetic
Dreamy	Apprehensive
Eager	Distraught
Encouraged	Disgusted
Energized	Dreading
Enthused	Frustrated
Excited	Gloomy
Happy	Hateful
Hopeful	Indifferent
Inspired	Irritated
Motivated	Lethargic
Moved	Nervous
Passionate	Restless
Raring to go	Sad
Stimulated	Scared
Stirred	Uneasy
Thrilled	Uninterested
Zestful	Unmotivated

Use this list as a guide to redirect and change the way you think about negative situations and personal states of being. If you are diligent, you will see that over time, it is really the way you allow yourself to perceive your world that dictates how your life will be.

Like our emotions, our bodies will also give us physical signals that are either positive or negative, if we are paying attention. Checking in with your body—doing a complete head to toe scan—will give you clues as to which direction you should go. Facial expression, physical attitude, posture and overall body language are all signals that can be deciphered. They hold valuable information and insight as to how you really feel or how you should proceed.

Positive Physical Signals	Negative Physical Signals
Arms at side	Arms crossed
Chin up	Chin down
Energetic face	Clenching teeth
Hands animated	Hands clasped
Leaning forward	Fidgeting
Loose muscle tone	Tight muscle tone
Paying attention	Looking away
Relaxed posture	Tense posture
Sitting up straight	Slouching
Smiling	Frowning
Speaking up clearly	Speaking soft or low
Warmth or sweating	Coldness or chills
Wide eyed	Uninterested

At first it may seem hard to know what you are feeling and why, especially if you have been taught that emotions are "weak" or "self-indulgent." But with thought, process and practice, you can become a master of your emotional guidance system. It will not steer you wrong. The trick is to always be proactive and control your outward responses. Using the following process will help you see more clearly what your emotions are telling you.

Making Decisions with a Mind-Map

For this process, you will need a pen or pencil, two different-colored highlighters, and a red pen, crayon or pencil. Use the provided process pages at the end of this chapter. We are going to create a mind-map of your challenge and the emotions surrounding it.

When faced with uncertainty about a choice, write your question down in the center of a blank sheet of paper. Then sit quietly for a few moments letting the essence of the situation sink in. Now check in with your mind and body. What does your inner sense say about the situation? What does your body language tell you? Do a complete emotional and physical scan of yourself, and randomly write down all of your feelings and sensations anywhere on the paper.

When you feel the process is finished, take one color highlighter (I like the yellow for this one) and outline all the *positive* signals. Now use the other color (perhaps the blue) to highlight all the *negative* sensations. The next step may be tricky—it requires a bit of thought and complete honesty with yourself. Look over your list of negatives and discern if any of these are really fears of following through and not purely emotional and physical signposts.

If it is something that you truly do not want to do, you will know this in the core of your being. If you get a totally negative feeling inside, this is a definite signal of "no" about whether or not you should follow through. If it is actually a fear, you will have a "but" attached to it. Whether the feeling is positive or negative, a "but" attached always signals some kind of fear you need to address and move through. The following example will show you the difference between feelings of a "no" and a "fear."

I was negotiating contracts with two different companies. Both firms represented themselves very well, and both seemed to have the talents and tools I needed. After my research was done, I still could not decide which company to hire for the job.

I put both contracts side by side on the table in my living room and let them sit there for a few days. I had trepidations about signing both contracts. I was very confused at that point. I had done all my homework, and these two companies looked the best. Perhaps I should find more to compare, I thought. I finally decided to take a deeper look inside myself and find out exactly why I was having such a problem with both firms.

I decided I had no fears about the first contract, but I had a "gut" feeling against signing it and sending in a deposit. It was not that I had a bad feeling about the people or the job they would do, I just felt I could find someone who understood me better and connect with exactly what I was trying to do. I knew then the first firm was not for me.

As I evaluated the second firm on my list, I noticed they were congruent with everything I actually wanted. Although they did not have the fancy marketing and corporate-looking forms of the first firm, I felt good about them. So why was I having problems making a decision? As I thought about it more, I realized that this firm would be able to do exactly what I wanted and bring me to where I wanted to go.

And *that* is what was fearful for me—not the fact that they would do a great job, but that I might actually be ultra-successful at my venture. When I looked at my feelings honestly, I saw my personal insecurities about my ability to perform, not theirs! After I figured out that it was my inner fears holding me back from hiring this particular company, I signed the contract and sent in my retainer. When I had signed the contract, they gave me more detailed information about the services and contacts they could offer me. I found out then that I had made a very important, correct decision.

Here is another example. I met a woman who expressed an interest in dating me. My first "gut" reaction was to say no because this woman, although very nice, would not be the best person for me to be involved with.

After I mulled it over for a few days, I thought maybe it would be okay after all. I told myself that I deserved to get out of the house more and date someone, no matter who it was. Even thought my intuition said to back off, I rationalized going ahead. I convinced myself it would be okay to pursue this woman romantically. The closer I began to get to her, the more red flags kept popping up. But I kept talking myself into the relationship and convincing myself I was just in fear of commitment. Was it really fear, or was it knowing this relationship would not serve me? As things turned out, it soon became obvious that I was not afraid of commitment but of a relationship I knew would end badly. I should have listened more closely to the negative signals my feelings were sending me.

Even though your mind may think logically about the potential advantages of the situation, deep down you will know that you will be unhappy about making it happen. Fear comes not necessarily from a negative mindset but from a pessimistic thought pattern. In order to discern the difference between negative signals and fear, remember this: Fear comes from how we are *thinking* and negative signals come from how we *feel*. If you absolutely know that this action or decision will be good for you and make you happy, then the negativism you feel is only fear. If you find that some of the negative emotional and physical signals you have written down are in fact fears, then put an "X" through those items using your red pen, following the example above. At the end of this process, you will have a mental picture on paper of the situation and how you feel about it.

If you have more yellow-highlighted positive signals, then the answer to your choice is "yes." If you have more blue-highlighted negative signposts, then the answer is "no." Once you get accustomed to using this process on paper, you'll be able to do it quickly in your head without needing to see it written down. The more in touch you become with your inner guidance system, the quicker and easier it will be to make the right decisions about your life.

This process is definitely not limited to just major life decisions. You can check in anytime with your emotions regarding any situation, question or decision you have. If you are going to the gym, you inner spirit knows if you need weight training or cardio that day, so check in. At lunchtime, your body knows if salad or a chicken sandwich would be best. You'll even get information on what to wear and if you should bring a coat along that day. And yes, your inner signal system even will know if that new romantic interest is a good choice or not.

    Navigating your day using you inner signals and signposts will allow your life to flow harmoniously, bringing you toward what is truly good for you and steering you away from harmful situations. Learn to know, trust and follow your emotions, and creating the life you want and deserve will become much easier.

-Exercise 15-

An Exercise in Flow

For one entire day, listen to your inner voice and follow its lead. If you get a feeling or thought, then follow it to where it leads. At first, it may be best to try this exercise when you are not at work, but using your internal guide is very beneficial anywhere, anytime.

Start when you wake up in the morning. Do whatever you feel you should. Depart from your normal routine, and let your spirit guide you every step of the way. Do not fret about where you will end up; just go with the flow. This may be difficult at first, but trust yourself. Trust that within you is a base of wisdom and knowledge that has been put there solely for your benefit to enhance your existence on earth. Follow your heart, go on instinct; you may be pleasantly surprised at where you'll end up. Try it, and then write about your experience below. Have fun!

Elements of Life Success

David Michael Ferruolo

Feel Your Way Through with a Mind-Map

Question/Problem

Elements of Life Success

Feel Your Way Through with a Mind-Map

Question/Problem

David Michael Ferruolo

-Chapter 16-

Creating Affirmations

No book on manifesting life success would be complete without a chapter on affirmations. This technique is an incredibly powerful tool for keeping a positive mindset, staying focused on what you want and accepting what is to come as fact and not fantasy. By affirming to yourself daily the things you are doing and are capable of, you can direct your mindset towards the positive and the optimistic. If we can keep an upbeat, proactive attitude towards our pursuits, they will be more attainable, and we will have much more fun during our journey. Since we are in search of our dreams and goals during most of our waking lives, it is in our interest to master having a good attitude. By using affirmations, we can keep healthy attitudes and continually direct our thoughts towards positive outcomes.

Affirmations are merely statements that verify what we want, how we are doing and what we are capable of. They are short verses or sentences of empowerment that we routinely say to ourselves aloud or silently. They can be general or very specific, depending on our situations and what we are doing. Affirmations can target either qualities in ourselves or action steps we must take.

Generalized Affirmations:

I am an intelligent and capable person.
I am confident and determined.
I am compassionate and understanding.
I have the power to manifest success in my life.
I bring into my life easily all that I dream and desire.
My life is changing daily for the better.

Specific Affirmations:

I will receive the promotion I seek at work because I am the most qualified person.
I will eat only good, healthy foods that keep my mind, body and spirit strong.
I will learn to ski this winter.
By (insert date) I will have a new vehicle (insert specific type) to drive.
By (insert date) I will lose (insert number) pounds and will drop (insert number) waist sizes.
By (insert date) I will ask that interesting person for a date.

When writing affirmations, we should always phrase them in the positive. We always ask for what we do want, not what we do not want! To keep your affirmations directed toward the positive, start them off with:

I am...
I have...
I bring...
I will...

And always follow up with something positive and proactive. Never use *"I am not,"* because this focuses your mind on a negative energy. Your affirmation should be positive and optimistic. This may feel very odd to you because it is so common to be negatively reinforced in today's society. Daily we hear what bad will happen to us if we do not do something. The old "if-then" scenario—it is used on us and we in turn use it on others:

Negative Scenarios:

If you don't show up for work, then you'll get fired.
If you don't stop smoking, then you'll die of lung cancer.
If you don't take out the trash, then you'll be grounded.
If you don't lose 15 pounds, then you'll never get a date.
If you don't do this good thing, then this bad thing will happen to you.

Negative reinforcement creates dissonance and friction. Nobody likes to be told what to do or be given an ultimatum. This can create rebellion as well as lead to self-destructive habits. People can become trapped and paralyzed because they fear all the negative things that could happen to them. So sometimes they give up and settle for a lesser life, or sometimes they become focused on perfection and burn out. It is very unhealthy to pursue an objective for

Elements of Life Success

negative reasons. It is much healthier and much more fun if we have confident, constructive reasons to complete a task.

Positive Scenarios:

If you show up for work every day, you'll be considered for a raise.
If you stop smoking, you'll breathe easier and have a more enjoyable life.
If you take out the trash every Thursday, you'll make me very happy and prove that you are a capable, responsible person.
If you lose 15 pounds, you'll be more attractive to the opposite sex.
If you do this good thing, then this better thing will happen!

When there is a positive outcome associated with a project or task, we instinctively want to commit to doing it. Most people like rewards better than punishment, and we have to treat ourselves accordingly. We have to talk to ourselves with a positive tone and picture the benefits. Positive affirmations work because they empower, uplift and motivate us. They are always upbeat and encouraging.

Affirmations are better written in the now than in a speculative time frame. You need to accept that things are happening in your life now, not some speculative time in the future. Do not get "being in the now" confused with making deadlines and goal dates in your affirmations. For instance do not start an affirmation with "someday I will..." or "soon this will happen to me." Make them definitive, as if everything is happening now. Just remember, now is the only time we command, now is the time we have total control over, so voice your affirmations in the now. They will be much more powerful, potent and energetic.

Write Your Affirmations

When producing affirmations, you should have your goal lists, pen or pencil, and seven 3x5 index cards, or cut seven 3x5 pieces of paper from a larger sheet. You can also use the exercise sheet at the end of this chapter as a guide. Your task is to generate at least 21 concrete affirmations based on your goals, encompassing who you are, where you are going and what you want. Like your goals, your affirmations are alive and should be revised as often as you feel the need. On each of the seven cards, start by writing this list three times in a row:

I am...
I bring...
I have...
I will...

First, look over your goal lists. Think about who you will have to become, in order to be the person who can accomplish these life desires. What has to change? What has to come into your life? How do you want to be, to look, to act? Think of your character, values and morals, as well as what has to happen and by what target date.

Then, go back to your process cards, look at the first *"I am..."* and complete a positive affirmation.

Elements of Life Success

Now, go on to the next *"I bring," "I have,"* and *"I will,"* and write more positive affirmations. Once you find the flow, write out at least 21 positive affirmations. You can start with the suggested words above, or you can make up different phrasings, but make sure you always write them in the positive and in the now.

When you are finished, look over your affirmation list and see how it feels. If you need to make a few revisions, additions or subtractions, please do so now. You should have at least 21 concrete, positive affirmations on your index cards to use in your daily life. Feel free to create as many more affirmation cards as you think you need. Trust your instincts to guide you to the correct number.

You should carry these affirmation cards with you daily, and, at least three times a day, take out one of the cards and read it. Every morning when you wake and every evening before you sleep are great times to use your affirmation cards. During the day, it is easy to reach into your pocket, backpack or purse and pull out a card.

Speaking your affirmations aloud is very powerful and should be done as often as you are able. Maybe it has something to do with the vibrations that you send out to the universe, or maybe it just feels good to hear it aloud. Whatever the reason, I know that saying them aloud is very motivating and uplifting. Stand up and try it right now.

I am a powerful and beautiful person.
I will achieve all my goals and live the life of my dreams.

David Michael Ferruolo

I bring into my life easily all that I need and desire.
I have a life of harmony, happiness and abundance.

Now, do it again but louder. In fact, yell them as loud as you can! How does it feel to profess to the world your intentions and your character? This can have a tremendous positive effect on your drive and determination. Keep your affirmation cards with you, and look them over as often as you can. When you are able, say them aloud. You can also look in the mirror and say your affirmations to yourself.

Another great technique is to work with a partner who has a list of his or her own affirmations. Sit or stand across from your partner with nothing in between. It will help if you are facing each other and holding hands, though this is not necessary. The first person will read or say one affirmation from his list. As you do this, look directly into your partner's eyes. Hold your gaze on her and do not look away. With as much feeling as you can, speak your affirmation to your partner. Now your partner will, in turn, affirm back to you what you said to her by saying "Yes, you are..." Your partner will speak with feeling and look directly into your eyes when doing so.

Person #1: *"I am a powerful and beautiful person."*
Person #2: *"Yes, (use first name), you are a powerful and beautiful person."*

Each of you selects three affirmations to share and affirm with the other. Affirmations are very powerful tools for motivation, encouragement and keeping a positive outlook.

I know that they work, and I encourage you to try them for yourself.

Visualize Your Success

Having a clear vision of what is to come and being able to see yourself succeeding in your endeavors can have an awesome positive effect on your attitude and outlook. Visualization is nothing more than controlled, directed daydreams. Instead of dreaming about what *would* be nice to achieve, or the *potential* positive outcome of a situation, you imagine in detail how nice it will be *when* you succeed and *when* the situation turns out positively for you.

Visualization can be used for any reason and any situation. But unlike a daydream, where the movie in your head takes random paths, you consciously direct each scene of your visualization to turn out exactly as you want it to be. You can even take it one step further by writing out your visualization on paper as a short story.

Can you create in your mind a vivid, detailed picture of what you want your future to look like? Do you have the ability to "walk through" or "play out" an upcoming situation and see the positive outcome? If you can do this, you are already visualizing. Here's how the process works:

Direct Your Daydreaming: This visualization technique is very simple and can be learned and refined easily. At first, you may find it hard to concentrate, but with practice it becomes easy to cultivate. When you first begin working with this process, you may want to find a quiet place. After a while, you will be able to conjure up positive images in your mind easily and quickly, no matter where you are or what is going on around you.

Relaxing Is the First Step: Whether you are standing, sitting or lying down, you have to be calm and quiet. You may keep your eyes open or close them, but be careful not to fall asleep during this process. We are merely practicing a form of meditation, so do your best to stay awake. Take a deep breath and put a smile on your face. As you let the breath out, relax your entire body from head to toe. Take several more breaths and make the relaxation complete.

Start Thinking: Breathe gently, keep the smile on your face and start thinking about your perfect future. Just let the thoughts pop in and out of your mind randomly for a few moments. Think of your goal lists if you have completed them. What will your career be like? Your home life? Your lifestyle? And your personal self? In a perfect world, how will these be? Let the thoughts come and go as they will.

Create Your Pictures: Then start purposely directing and holding your thoughts on one particular item or situation, such as your home, family or office. Start creating images of the surroundings and the things in your perfect life. But start with a bird's-eye view, from afar, and very slowly work your way in. This may be as far as you get at first, but keep practicing. It will eventually become very clear and vivid. As you work your way in to a closer view, create all the important details. Like editing a movie, mentally piece together the pictures in your mind to seem as if you are walking through your future life right now. See, feel, taste and smell everything around you. The more vivid you can make it, and the more senses you can bring into play, the more powerful the process will be.

Save the File*:* After a brief time of visualization, save the images so that you can access them again. You can mentally place them in a box and set them on a shelf in your mind; you can imagine your brain as a computer and simply hit the save button; or you can journal your experience for future use. Your visualizations are always a work in progress, and the more you practice and remember them, the more vivid and powerful they will become.

Savor the Moment*:* As you come out of your daydream, savor the essence of how good it was to be in your perfect world. Know that this place is a pending reality—it will happen as the result of your hard work and determination. Remember that thought is the energy of manifestation and the seed of all creation. If we can think it, it can happen.

Whether a business meeting, a judo match, a final exam or a first date, you can use this process of visualization to create a positive atmosphere, preserve a healthy attitude and relax your butterflies! It can also greatly center you so that you can remember your goals and keep your focus. The process is the same as above, except you focus on a specific situation and see the outcome as you would like it to be.

Experiment with Advanced Techniques

Visionary Writing: Some people have a greater propensity for writing out a detailed story than actually visualizing it in their minds. Visionary writing is a great tool for the creative mind to tell the story of a desired future or situational outcome. Just find some quiet time alone, and write or type out a creative, descriptive story of your life or a pending situation. Write from a place of optimism, and always present the work in the positive. Always portray yourself in the best possible situation with the best possible realistic outcome. The story can be as short or long as you like, but it should read like a fairy tale and have a great ending.

Visual Collage: A visual collage is nothing more than actual pictures of what you want, pasted on a piece of paper or poster board. It may be as simple as one photo with some writing on it or as in-depth as many photos overlaid to create a large poster. One of my all-time favorites for this exercise is the multi-picture frame with cut-outs for many photos, which is available in most discount stores.

Find a multi-photo frame with six or more places for pictures. Take photographs with your own camera, or find pictures in a magazine of what you want in life. Post the photos in the frame's cut-out spaces, and hang it in your home where you can see it often. There is a great power in having a few pictures of what you want posted in strategic places. Be creative with this process and have fun with it.

Some effective placements of your photos could be: Paste a photo of yourself next to your dream car and tape it up on the garage door. Cut your head out of a photograph of yourself and paste it on a body you like from a health magazine—tape this picture in the bathroom or on the refrigerator. Find photos of the kind of home you want and tape them to the bedroom door. These are only a few suggestions of what you can do--feel free to expand them. These visual reminders will keep your mind focused on your goal and help direct your life in the right direction.

Lucid Dreaming: I mention lucid dreaming here because, when practicing visualization and directed daydreaming, you might sometimes fall asleep—but you can learn to continue the visualization in your subconscious mind. This can sometimes cause you to feel alarmed if you are not ready for it, because you feel as if you are living your thoughts but have no body control. You are actually in a very light state of slumber, so you are slightly aware but sleeping at the same time. When you find yourself going into a lucid dreaming state, you can sometimes scare yourself awake, only to wish you had not. Getting back to that state can prove difficult, but it is well worth it. If you find yourself able to experience lucid dreaming, please seek out more information on the subject. It is a very powerful process and well worth your effort.

Once you are well practiced in these creative visualization techniques, you will be able to turn them on and off at will. Just be careful not to let your visualizations turn into unrealistic fantasies. Stay true to your goals and your life purpose, and these techniques will help produce amazing outcomes in your life.

-Exercise 16-

Creating Affirmations

Career Affirmations:

-
-
-
-
-

Family Affirmations:

-
-
-
-
-

Elements of Life Success

Personal Affirmations:

-
-
-
-
-

Lifestyle Affirmations:

-
-
-
-
-

David Michael Ferruolo

-Chapter 17-

The Difference Between Thinking and Knowing

All the people I have met or read about who have accomplished anything of substance, including myself, did not just believe they could do it—they knew they could. Have you ever noticed that when you ask someone about their amazing accomplishments, most respond with something like, "It was tough, but I knew I could do it."

There is such truth to that. Knowing cancels out all doubt and insecurity. There is no fear when you know that you will accomplish something. Trepidation comes only with the uncertainty of *thinking* that you have the ability to pull something off, not *knowing* that you can. When you *only think* you can do something, you can *only try* to do it. When there is *knowing* about your aptitudes and capabilities in your heart and soul, you do not try—you do. In the words of Master Jedi Yoda, from the motion picture series *Star Wars*, "Do, or do not. There is no try."

There is great wisdom in that statement. If you only try to accomplish something, you are not really doing it.

Elements of Life Success

Your mind and spirit are not 100 percent in it, and you inevitably have fear and doubt concerning the outcome. When you only try, you always leave a space in your mind for failure. Trying means you are not sure of yourself, so you had better think about the contingencies. By committing to only trying, you anticipate failure and provide a reason for not taking steps toward your dreams as valid options. Trying is a characteristic of not knowing yourself and what you are capable of.

Failure, on the other hand, is not an option when you fully commit to doing something. When you say, "I will do this," you know and commit to a definite outcome. When you are definitive and decisive in thought and action, you do not think of contingencies or failure as possibilities. Instead, you totally dedicate yourself to the desired outcome. *Doing* is a characteristic of confident, well-defined people. People who *do* are committed, determined and full of energy because they know they will achieve their goals, do it with ease and move rapidly toward the life of their dreams.

So if the future is always entirely unwritten and uncertain, how can we ever be sure and confident that the outcome will be in our favor? First, we have to separate knowing we *can* do something and knowing *how* something will turn out. We can never know how something will turn out, but we can embrace the uncertainty of the future as the greatest adventure and challenge we will have. We have no control over the future and how things will play out, but we can know ourselves and be confident in our abilities. This is what to focus on: your commitment and your capabilities.

Knowing you can accomplish something comes from having a core belief in yourself and a trust in a greater power. Couple this trusting belief with well-defined goals for your life and the ability to create an action plan, and you will be on your way to Life Success. When those special people say, "I will *do* that," they are 100 percent confident in their ability to set that goal and follow their action plan to fruition. They do not know the future anymore than you or I do, but they believe in themselves and trust in their abilities to create, plan and follow through. This is what anyone must concentrate on to achieve lofty goals.

Many people get caught up in the hugeness, the monstrosity, of the tasks that lie ahead of them. They concentrate on their uncertainties about the future rather than on what they can control in the present. Fear and doubt will set in if you try to predict the future or control others around you, so focus on the tasks you do control—defining your life, setting goals, creating an action plan, overcoming obstacles, and enjoying your life! Choose the action plan which best propels you toward your goals. Do not concern yourself with what you cannot control. Take action and make the tough choices to change your life for the better. Always remember to have fun and enjoy yourself along the way—attainment is momentary, but the path is infinite.

Here are some ways to tell the difference between what we think and what we know. Study the chart on the next page and see if you are in the thinking or the knowing. Know if you change your thoughts via the words you use, your mindset will follow. The interesting thing about the mind is that it creates its reality out of what you tell it too!

Thinking	Knowing
Is frequently uncertain	Has certainty
Has doubts	Has conviction
Can be fearful	Is empowering
Has no definite outcome	Has a definite outcome
Lacks vision	Has clear vision
Has worries	Is confident
Means winging it	Means an action plan
Is associated with:	Is associated with:
If	Yes
Maybe	Definitely
Try	Do
Attempt	Complete
We'll see	Success
I don't know	Achieve
I'm not sure	No problem
I hope	I know
I wish	I will
I might	I can

When you are in a mindset of knowing, it will feel different—and good. You will feel empowered to take action, and you will have a confident vision of completion. You will be eager and full of energy, ready to take action. There will be excitement and commitment as you face the tasks at hand. There will be a clear-cut goal with definite action steps. You will have an overall feeling of well-being, a sense of the accomplishment as if it had already happened.

When our thoughts are centered only on thinking we might be able, we become very uncertain. Fear sets in because we doubt our abilities to follow through. The path gets hazy with no clear direction. We will be sluggish and reluctant to go forth, and the task will seem out of reach and overwhelming. Our energy will be low, and we will have an overall poor feeling associated with the entire endeavor. Even trying will be a stretch, as we subconsciously make plans to fail and not carry through.

Stay in touch with your feelings and emotions. When you start feeling less than confident, pull back and evaluate your thinking. If you find you are thinking of things that are out of your control, bring your thoughts back to the certainties of what you know. Use affirmations and meditation. Stay focused on the present, and apply thought and action to what you can do now. Learning to tell which train of thought you are experiencing is very important to your overall attitude and success. For when you *know* you are able, you will be able to follow through. Have faith in yourself and your abilities, and trust and know that you can make it happen. You can create your destiny. It only takes proper thought and right action.

-Exercise 17A-

A Reality Check

How "knowing" are you about your ability to follow through with your dreams? It is time to rate yourself. In the box below, list six of your most important dreams and rate them as to whether you are unsure or knowing. Be honest with yourself. If you are completely certain, circle the number 5 on the far right of the knowing side. If you are totally unsure of yourself, circle the 5 on the left of the thinking side. If you are somewhere in between, circle the number you feel accurately sums up where you are.

Goal	Thinking or Knowing
(1)	5 4 3 2 1 0 1 2 3 4 5
(2)	5 4 3 2 1 0 1 2 3 4 5
(3)	5 4 3 2 1 0 1 2 3 4 5
(4)	5 4 3 2 1 0 1 2 3 4 5
(5)	5 4 3 2 1 0 1 2 3 4 5
(6)	5 4 3 2 1 0 1 2 3 4 5

What is your overall impression? Are you mostly in the knowing or are you uncertain? Write about how you feel.

....

....

....

....

David Michael Ferruolo

-Exercise 17B-
Change Your Thoughts from Thinking to Knowing

For each of the six goals you listed above, write about why you are not completely in the knowing side of the chart. What are your fears and insecurities about each goal?

Goal 1) _____

_____

_____

_____

_____

_____

_____

Goal 2) _____

_____

_____

_____

_____

_____

Goal 3) _____

_____

_____

_____

_____

_____

Goal 4)_____

_____

_____

_____

_____

Goal 5)_____

_____

_____

_____

_____

Goal 6)_____

_____

_____

_____

_____

Now it is time to rewrite your uncertainty mind-script. Write a life script stating how it would be and how it would feel if you were confident and knew you had the ability to bring forth your dreams. Describe what might take place if you believed in yourself and trusted in your guiding power. Are there really any valid, concrete reasons for you to only think you can and not know you will succeed?

David Michael Ferruolo

If you do have a valid obstacle, then refer back to Chapter 14, "Overcoming Obstacles." If you do have a valid fear, refer back to Chapter 13, "Overcoming Fears." If you are unsure of a decision, refer back to Chapter 15. "Feel Your Way Through," and if you are unsure of where to start, refer back to Chapter 12, "Take Action." All the information you need to get your mindset into the knowing mode is in this book. Refer back to the chapters you need to move out of thinking and into knowing. Write about it below.

David Michael Ferruolo

-Chapter 18-

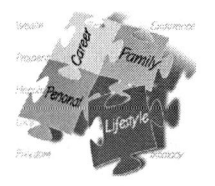

The Value of Support

In order to create true Life Success and start thriving in the world, you need a lot of help and support along the way. You may be capable of many things, but sooner or later, without help from someone else, you will end your journey short of the destination. Many people like to use the words "independent" or "autonomous" to describe themselves. To a small degree they may be, but if we were to take a deeper look into the circumstances of their lives, it would reveal how dependent they are on others.

Think of all the thousands of people it takes to support our daily lives. How could we even eat if it weren't for the growers, packers, shippers, truckers, inspectors, stockers, and cashiers? Just take the simple example of a gallon of milk, and imagine all the hands that it takes to get that gallon of milk into your home. Look around and think of how many people have a hand in your daily life. If you possess even one utensil, linen, weapon, pan or piece of clothing that you did not make yourself, you have counted on someone else to make your survival possible. Yes, we are responsible for our own life directions and have to make our own decisions, but the world we live in is completely interdependent. Anyone who says he or she can go it alone does not see the whole picture of human interdependence accurately.

When we finally realize that our destiny is thoroughly contingent on the help and support of others, we will start enlisting and welcoming more people into our lives. Our walls of perceived protection will come down when we accept the reality and inevitability of others playing key roles in our lives.

The quality of people in your support system is very important. To have a high-quality life, there have to be high-quality people supporting it. Picking the right people to be in your life as you climb the ladder of your life success is a crucial decision, and a tough one. The quality of people around you will dictate the quality of the end result. You must choose wisely.

The problem is, most of us do not know whom we need and what we need them to do, until we are faced with a difficult situation. When this happens, we usually grasp at straws, picking the most convenient person to fill the position. These hasty decisions may lead to unnecessary challenges or postponements of your goals, when you realize that the person you chose is not the right one for the job. To avoid pitfalls, disappointments and failures, we must think ahead to identify the type of person(s) we need most, and then determine what they will do for us, just as we did when setting our goals and making our action plans.

What Kinds of People Do You Need?

Within each of your four goal categories – career, family, personal and lifestyle – there will be a few important supporting people who will be instrumental to your success. It is essential to think ahead about what kinds of people these should be, so that you can choose the right person when the time comes, or recognize them when you cross paths. Within each goal category, you should outline all the supporting jobs and tasks that will have to be done by other people, groups or companies.

For instance, if you are writing a book, you will need: experts on your topic, a writers' support group, an editor, an agent, a publisher, a publicist and a timely pizza delivery man, to name only a few. To know what kinds of people you need is a great start, but then you must take it one step further and imagine the attributes, character traits, skills, values, morals and personality that would make this person the perfect pick for a supporting role in your life. When choosing a company, think of its philosophy, history, integrity and vision. As we did with our goals, we need to think of the best-case or "dream" scenario.

When I found myself a single parent, I knew I was in hot water. How was I going to be able to run my businesses and still raise my son? I had joint custody, and he was with me 50 percent of the time. This made it tough to get any work done and also created internal stress. The work was piling up at my business, jobs were not getting done, contracts were being lost, bills were going unpaid and, in the process, I was losing money. I was in trouble and I did not know how I was going to get myself out of it. Notice all the "I"s in the previous sentence?

Up to that point in my life I had not learned the lesson of asking for help or looking for support. I had done everything myself. I ran my business alone and did all the work myself—all of it. Sales, labor, service, accounting, merchandising, maintenance—these were the hats I wore on a daily basis. I worked 60 to 70 hours, seven days a week, but now I had my son to take care of as well. My work productivity was cut in half, as was my paycheck. I had to make some hard choices. I decided it was more important for me to be with my boy than to continue working, but to do this I would need help, and I would have to relinquish most of the control I had over my business to others.

I made a list of key career-related people I needed to help run my business, plus all the attributes they had to have to keep it successful. My search was for only two key people: first, a good salesperson to work the shop, and second, a great scuba-diving instructor to take care of all the classes. As I interviewed people for the positions, I kept my list of desirable attributes close by. There were many qualified applicants, but finding one with the right character traits was difficult. Nevertheless, I trusted it all would work out and meditated daily on finding the right people.

During my meditation I would visualize what my shop would look like with these two people working there, and without me. I made myself imagine how smoothly things were going, and how all the contracts, students and bills were easily taken care of. I visualized the weekly sales logs growing and thought of the profits that would be generated.

I set my intention on finding the right persons, and like magic, one appeared.

A former student walked into my shop one day in late winter. As we talked about her college experience and her love of scuba diving, I knew she was the right person for the job. I asked her if she wanted a full-time summer job, and she accepted. This was the best thing that ever happened to my business and my personal life. She proved to be more than amazing and generated more sales than I had projected. And although I did not find the scuba-diving instructor, my new salesperson did so much great work I was able to handle the class load myself. That was the best and most profitable year of business I have ever had.

Finding the right support person or people can make the difference between succeeding or failing. It is up to us to realize we cannot go the road alone, and we need supportive, helpful people in our lives. Finding willing people is easy, but finding the right people takes much thought, energy and patience. I would suggest not being hasty in your choices, but make sure you have thought over all your candidates thoroughly. No matter if it is an employee, a business partner, a mechanic for you car, a daycare provider, or even a romantic partner, make sure the person you choose is truly Mr. or Ms. Right, and not Mr. or Ms. Right-Now.

Career Support People

As you look over your career goal list, think of all the people, groups and businesses that you will need to deal with in the pursuit of your dreams. Go slowly. Take time to think through each career goal thoroughly. Who will be the key players, the springboards, the foundations of your newly planned life? It is your task to identify the most significant kinds of people that you will need to get where you are going. List as many as you can think of on the "Career Support People" page at the end of this chapter. Once you are done, review the list and make modifications as needed.

Now let's think of what you want these selected people-positions to be like. What would be their ideal attributes, character traits, values, morals, views on life and personalities? You want to end up with a general list of the most desirable core traits. These traits will be common to all the areas of life throughout your search for the actual right persons. Individual skills and knowledge will differ, but overall, their character traits will be similar.

Desirable Core Traits

Now you can create a list—using a word, phrase or sentence—to describe all the attributes of those whom you would like to have supporting you with your career goals. Some common traits could be:

Assertive	Intelligent
Beneficial	Joyful
Calm	Knowledgeable
Cheerful	Loyal
Commanding	Methodical
Communicative	Optimistic
Concise	Passionate

Decisive	Realistic
Detail-oriented	Respectful
Determined	Spiritual
Elegant	Stern
Energetic	Truthful
Flexible	Visionary
Hard-working	Wise

Once you have finished your list of career support people and the attributes you feel they must have, move on to people for your other areas of life—personal, family, lifestyle—and create similar lists, using the worksheets at the end of this chapter. For each category make a detailed list of attributes you want these people to have. Don't forget to think about personality, character, morals and values. The more detailed you get, the better you will be able to see the kinds of people you want in your life. This is powerful information to know, and it will help you greatly in finding the right person for the positions you need. It will also be valuable in keeping you from getting partnered or involved with the wrong person. So, again, take your time. Think clearly about where you want to go and the people you want near you on the way.

-Exercise 18-

Finding Your Support Network

Career Support People
Desirable Core Traits

Position: _____   Position: _____
-
-
-
-
-
-
-
-
-
-

Position: _____   Position: _____
-
-
-
-
-
-
-
-

David Michael Ferruolo

Family Support People
Desirable Core Traits

Position: _____   Position: _____

-
-
-
-
-
-
-
-
-

Position: _____   Position: _____

-
-
-
-
-
-
-
-
-

Elements of Life Success

Personal Support People
Desirable Core Traits

Position: _____   Position: _____
-
-
-
-
-
-
-
-
-

Position: _____   Position: _____
-
-
-
-
-
-
-
-
-

David Michael Ferruolo

Lifestyle Support People
Desirable Core Traits

Position: _____   Position: _____

-
-
-
-
-
-
-
-
-

Position: _____   Position: _____

-
-
-
-
-
-
-
-
-

Elements of Life Success

David Michael Ferruolo

- Chapter 19 -

Invincible Determination

I woke up in a daze. My head was pounding and I could barely move my legs and arms. My whole body ached—drained completely and sore from head to toe. The sun coming in the window hurt my eyes, so I kept them shut. Squinting, I tried to see where I was—I could not remember. A bed of some sort? The hospital? I had no idea. The only thing I knew for sure was the pain I felt.

I opened my mouth to speak. My lips were dry and my throat parched. Forcing air up through my larynx, I attempted a hello to see if anyone was there, but only a weak moaning sound materialized. I heard something...or someone. "Hey man, you're awake. Wow, you've been out for over 30 hours. How do you feel?"

What the hell, I thought, where am I? Okay, what was the last thing I remembered? Then it all came back to me...and in my mind I heard those words—the words I'll never forget even to this day: "Boat Crew, you are secured from Hell Week. Congratulations!" Tears formed in my eyes and I found the strength to sit up. "I did it!" I said, looking around to see that I was in my barracks room in the BUDs compound at the Naval Amphibious Base in Coronado, California. I looked at the other bunks to see my friends who also had endured those horrendous seven days of non-stop, well, hell. An officer whom I did not know helped us to sit up and said he would get us to the chow hall because we must all be very hungry. I looked at my classmates and made eye contact with each of the other three men in my room. We smiled, and then we all started to laugh uncontrollably. Someone yelled, "HooYa, Class 141!"

Just then one of the SEAL instructors came into our room. He peered at us for a moment, his handlebar mustache hanging over his maniacal smirk. The smiles quickly vanished from our faces as he said, "What the hell are you ladies so happy for? You think you are done? You think you did something special? You made it through the first 5 weeks of training—big deal. You still have 21 weeks to go. You think Hell Week was tough? Well, we are just getting started!"

As quickly as he came, he vanished. When we were sure he was gone, the laughter broke out again. We all knew what we had accomplished, and of course we knew the next 21 weeks would be very tough. But there was a difference in my mind—in everyone's mind. It took will, it took determination, it took digging deeper into myself than I ever knew possible, but I—we all—made it through Hell Week, and I knew it was a defining accomplishment in all our lives. I knew I would never be the same, never think the same and never look at life the same way again.

David Michael Ferruolo

It had been five weeks of physical and mental torture. It had been five weeks of pain and uncertainty, of thinking about quitting, and of questioning my original decision to become a SEAL. But there was a difference now. In my mind I knew, without a shadow of a doubt, that I would someday wear the revered Trident pin that designates a Navy SEAL.

I had been tested and pushed beyond my limits hundreds of times in the past month. At first I did not know if I could handle it, but I hung in there. As time passed, I became more comfortable with my abilities, my performances and going beyond my perceived limitations. My doubts slowly became my convictions, and my insecurities my strengths. Through this time of trial, I transformed my mindset from fear and despair to an invincible determination. I knew the next 21 weeks would be tough, but I also knew I would be able to handle anything they threw at me. I had no doubt anymore that I would finish BUDs training and go on to be a SEAL.

At that point, sitting laughing on my bunk, I knew all the components of my life had come together for this single pursuit. I was now unshakable. I finally believed in my abilities, and I completely trusted that I was on my chosen path. I felt a new strength and power blossom within me, and my passion for being a SEAL became stronger than ever before. I had reawakened something from deep within my soul, and now my resolve was unwavering, my determination invincible. I was no longer just striving to "make it" — I had made "making it" my way of life.

Elements of Life Success

I am a firm believer that if you set your mind to doing something, it will be done. When all the pieces of your life's puzzle fit together snugly, and you are determined and unwavering in your commitment to succeed, you will. Every successful lifestyle is marked with determination, fortitude and tenacity. Many of the most successful people in the world attribute their success to their resolve. In the 1800s, Louis Pasteur, who unraveled the mysteries of many illnesses and contributed to the development of the first vaccines for rabies, anthrax and cholera, once said: *"Let me tell you the secret that has led me to my goal: my strength lies solely in my tenacity."*

Yet a life of achievement is more than a simple decision you can make; it is a complete lifestyle change. It is more than just physical actions on your part that will take you through the motions. Achievement must become second nature and accomplishment a habit. The difference between those who do and do not succeed in life is the level of belief and commitment they possess. Like Louis Pasteur, you must make tenacity a habit that you live by.

If you truly believe in yourself, your vision and what you are capable of, you can slowly start to ingrain the habit of a successful lifestyle within you.

This may seem like a hard thing to learn. However, it is more accurately something we must *learn to remember*—something that we all were born with but have suppressed. The suppression of these attributes starts at birth, unfortunately. We are all born with a winning attitude—that indomitable instinct to get what we want and must have to survive. But as we get older and are trained to adhere to the rules of society, it diminishes. We then inadvertently pass on this sense of caution and uncertainty to our children by continually saying "No" to their desires and by punishing them for their continual persistence.

I have learned this fact by observing my own son. From a very young age, perhaps 12 months, he knew exactly what he wanted and was tenacious in his quest to get it. Whether it was a new Thomas the Train toy or watching his favorite TV show, he was relentless in his pursuits. Lately his fascination is with a toy called Transformers.

Now at age four, he has the ability to incorporate his desire for getting more of these toys into almost every interaction he has with me. He'll tell me it is a good idea for us to go to Target or Wal-Mart because we are running low on dish soap or toilet paper. Of course, when we arrive, his next sentence will be to let me know that he will be going to "just look" at the Transformer toys.

If this tactic fails, which it does most days, he then will come and sit near me as I write. He'll bring one of his toys with him and play quietly for a moment. Then he'll mention how cool and educational his Transformers are, and wouldn't it be a good idea to have more? This will make him smarter, he proclaims. And when that fails, he will ask how many days until his birthday or Christmas, depending on the time of year. He then will bring down his list of Transformer toys and just casually remind me of the ones he does not yet have. This goes on all day—all day! His ability to incorporate his desires into any situation is uncanny, but it is completely natural.

I believe every child has this mindset—is born with it. If you do not agree, or do not have any kids of your own, go to a store and watch the families there. Most often you hear frustrated parents saying "No" and children crying. But through their tears and over the parent's stern "No," they relentlessly continue to ask for what they want.

In my casual observations, this quality is squelched somewhere between the ages of five and eight, depending on the character of the child. This characteristic, which is loathed by parents across the globe, may actually be one of our most valuable success attributes. But for most people, this treasure has gotten buried deep within us somewhere. Yet it is never truly gone—just repressed.

If it were completely gone, we would never want better lives. If it totally disappeared, we would be satisfied with mediocrity. If it were not still lingering, we would not feel frustrated and unfulfilled. This power of invincible determination lies within each and every one of us. We just have to reawaken its spirit and reincorporate it back into our lives. To achieve true Life Success, we must recapture and relearn the innocence, the enthusiasm and the tenacity we all once had as children. We have to dig deep within our souls and unearth the treasure-chest of success attributes that we were all born with.

Within this buried cache are some other unique but lost qualities. Along with tenacity, there is belief. And trust. And vitality. And passion. In fact, these five ingredients are the core components of invincible determination and must be unleashed if you are to achieve your own Life Success.

David Michael Ferruolo

Mahatma Gandhi said: *"Strength does not come from physical capacity. It comes from an indomitable will."*

When you can again believe that life is magical and limitless, when you can again trust in yourself and your guiding higher power, energy and inner strength will come alive within you. A passion will then burn for what you want and how you want to live. You do not have to go through Hell Week to unleash this power; you only have to commit to the process of renewal and change.

Remember: If you can change the way you think about your life, your life will change. When in your mind the only option is to follow through, then the only outcome can be success. In doing this, you will realize that happily seeking all the experiences life has to offer will ultimately fulfill your soul. And when this finally sinks into your head and your heart, every day of your life will lead to happiness, to achievement, and ultimately to Life Success.

-Exercise 19-

Are You Ready?

Ralph Waldo Emerson said, *"What lies behind us and what lies before us are small matters compared to what lies within us."* What lies within you, buried within the depths of your soul, your character and your spirit? Are you ready to unleash it? Are you ready to embrace your hidden inner power? Are you ready to meet your Life Success?

Write a proclamation to yourself, the world and the universe that states you are ready to unchain your hidden potential and pursue your dreams. Write about what kind of power lies within you, and how it will propel you towards success. Make this a promise to yourself, and a decree of your commitment to the future you will begin to create!

_____

_____

_____

_____

_____

_____

_____

David Michael Ferruolo

Elements of Life Success

David Michael Ferruolo

– Chapter 20 –

You Can Make It Happen!

I sometimes wonder what my life would be like if I hadn't taken the chances that I did, or hadn't made the necessary changes to follow my bliss. Where would I be, and what would I be doing now? I'm not sure, but I am certain I would be unhappy and unfulfilled. At these times I think about the words of George Sheehan: *"Success means having the courage, the determination, and the will to become the person you believe you were meant to be."*

I loved being a Navy SEAL, but I did not like military life. I was very stressed out and on edge all the time. It was safe and secure being in the military. I knew every day that I was going to eat and every week that I was going to get a paycheck. My life was planned out for me in the form of orders and operational plans. It was safe—but miserable. On the other hand, civilian life seemed very uncertain. What would I do? Where would I live? I did not have the answers, but I knew I had to leave—and so I did.

After being out for a while, as you may remember from my earlier comments, I took jobs as a landscaper and as a scuba shop manager before I found my way to more schooling. I had always wanted to be a musician, so I went to music school. I had no money, no job and no friends where I was going, but I went anyway. As well as I knew I had to leave the military, I also knew I could not stay in New England. Leaving the security of family and close friends, I again changed my life to follow my heart.

During my next phase, growing my hair long and playing in rock bands was one of the most invigorating things I had ever done in my life. Being on stage was like utopia for me. I loved every minute of that part of my life. The experience and friends will live on forever in my mind.

My saving grace during all these changes was discovering that somehow I have no problems facing the uncertainty of change. I found that living my life, being in charge of my path and taking control of my future was invigorating. I began to thrive on the challenge of change and achievement. For me, it was more important to be happy and fulfilled, following my dreams, than taking the safe, known road toward mediocrity. The thing is, I now know that at any time I can go and get that "normal" job and settle down somewhere. But that would not make me content—I would be miserable. I tried it, and I was.

After several years of music school, college, playing in bands and traveling around the country skiing, diving, rafting and having fun, I thought I should probably get a "real" job. So I moved back to New Hampshire and started a business. Again, with nothing but hopes and dreams, I opened my own scuba shop. It wasn't long after that I knew the life of a businessman was not for me. I was still unsatisfied and really wanted to leave and do something

David Michael Ferruolo

else, but I thought it was time to settle down and work for a living. For some, the scuba shop would have been a dream business, but I was not happy at all. Year after year I kept at it, and year after year I was dying inside. Like you, I knew there had to be something better, because many times in my life I had found it. After several years of searching, I finally found that my path was to become a writer and to let others learn from my hard-earned experiences.

So once again, with no concrete security in sight I set forth to change my life for the better. As I look back on this life, I am empowered by the knowledge that I have no regrets thus far. I have taken the chances, the blind leaps of faith, to propel my life on many adventures. I decided to trust in the power of the universe, and now I know God is always at my side. With optimism and zeal, I can look forward to every adventure this life has to offer.

You too can participate in this empowerment and this zest for life. During the course of reading this book, you have gained the tools to go forward with purpose, with energy, and with invincible determination.

Attaining the life you desire is not a goal but a lifestyle—a way of life. It is a style of living that continually focuses on a loftier vision of what your life can be. If you do go forward with this vision, your normal routines, daily habits and way of thinking will become aligned with where you want to go. The tug-of-war between what you say and what you do will stop. On the contrary, when your thoughts and actions work together with intention and determination, there is no limit to what you might accomplish. Your power to create the life you dream of is within you *right now*, begging to come out and help lead you down the road of success.

What about how difficult this all sounds? Wouldn't it be easier to just stay the way you are? Think hard: Will you be better off for not trying? Will you be happier if you maintain your current, known and safe path? And when your life has passed you by, what regrets will you feel if you do not at least give it a shot? Life is dynamic, full of change and uncertainty. Change is indeed the spice of life. Change is growth, and the alternative is stagnation and death. Are you ready to embrace life and take charge of your destiny?

You know now that your potential is unlimited—there is no end to what you can accomplish and achieve. Do not be fooled by the illusions of fear and doubt. Welcome the uncertainty of life, and know you are always in control of where you want to go. Life is an amazing adventure for those who choose make it so. With intent and determination, you can forge a path to everything you dream of and desire. Your destiny beckons, so what are you waiting for?

Are you ready to manifest your dreams in your real life? Are you ready to live amazingly? Are you ready to take that chance, walk that road, and see where it will take you? Are you ready to face the inevitable challenges and discover what you are made of? Are you ready to emerge, victorious?

Now it is all up to you. You have read carefully, thought well, and gathered all the tools necessary for you to go on. The rest of your life is your time to do with as you please. But always remember that the unfolding of "life" is your true destination, so savor it with every step. Focus on your dreams, live with enthusiasm and zeal, and enjoy every moment and every step of the way. There will be no exercise at the end of this chapter, because the next "exercise" is real life. Take what you have learned, and remember the words of Henry David Thoreau: *"If one advances confidently in the direction of his dreams, and endeavors to live the life which he has imagined, he will meet with a success unexpected in common hours."*

So get started today! I know that your life success awaits you, and I'll be with you in spirit all the way.

The Thank You Page

Writing and publishing a book is a daunting and extremely time-consuming project. The effort and energy that goes into producing the final product is amazing. This book would not be in the world if it were not for the help and support of the following great people.

I would like to thank Jennifer P. Crews for all her amazing insights, suggestions, support and love during the process of creating Life Success. Her incredible talents and input were invaluable. You are beautiful, and I love you.

Charlotte Cox, the editor who makes me look brilliant—Thank you. I am blessed to have you working with me, and I hope all our next projects will be as exciting and fun.

My amazing son, who at only 4, somehow knew the importance of my work. He quietly played beside me, day and night, as I plunged myself in this project. His temperament and patience are an inspiration. Thank you for being the greatest inspiration in my life.

I would also like to thank my Publicist, Cate Cummings for believing in me and putting up with my tenacious personality.

And to all the others, family and friend, (you know who you are)… thank you, thank you, thank you!

David Michael Ferruolo

David Michael Ferruolo

Lectures
Workshops
Book Signings
Speaking Engagements

For more information on Dave's schedule, please visit: www.daveferruolo.com

To schedule an event, please contact:

Mountain Lake Publishing
PO Box 6421
Laconia, NH 03246

(603) 556-4360 Voice
(603) 556-4361 Fax

info@mountainlakepublishing.com
www.mountainlakepublishing.com

www.daveferruolo.com

Elements of Life Success

Also Available from Dave Ferruolo

Connecting with the Bliss of Life
Powerful Lessons for Living a Peaceful & Happy Life

Special First Edition
ISBN 0-9767424-9-7

Available at:
www.DaveFerruolo.com
www.Amazon.com

About The Author

Dave Ferruolo has had a very active and interesting life. Born and raised in New England, he spent his childhood on the beaches of Rhode Island and in the mountains of New Hampshire.

His fascination with music began when his mother brought him to an Elvis Presley concert at age 10. A few years later, Dave got his first guitar and also found his second love—karate.

Enlisting in the Navy at 18, Dave was off to see the world. He volunteered for the Navy SEALs and successful completed the training. He became a member of SEAL Team 2 in Virginia Beach, VA, where he lived until his honorable discharge.

After the military, Dave perused his love of music at Music Tech in Minneapolis, MN. After a few years of college and playing in rock bands, he returned to NH and started his scuba diving business.

Dave still strums his guitars daily and runs his diving companies, but is now concentrating his time and efforts writing books and articles and touring the country speaking and facilitating workshops.

Dave's passion is inspiring others to connect with bliss and to achieve personal life success.

Suggestions for Further Reading

Carnegie, Dale. *How to Win Friends and Influence People*.
    New York: Pocket Books, 1936.

Covey, Stephen. *The 7 Habits of Highly Effective People*.
    New York: Simon & Schuster, 1989.

Dyer, Wayne W. *Inspiration: Your Ultimate Calling*.
    Carlsbad: Hay House, 2006.

Franklin, Benjamin. *The Art of Virtue*. Utah:
    Choice Skills, 1996.

Hemingway, Ernest. *The Old Man and the Sea*.
    New York: Scribner: Reissue Edition, 1995.

Hill, Napoleon. *Law of Success*. Los Angeles:
    Highroads Media, 2003.

Krishnamurti. *Think on These Things*. New York:
    Harper Perennial, 1989.

Lewis, Steven. *Sanctuary*. Los Angeles:
    HTT Press, LLC, 1998.

Mandino, Og. *The Choice*. New York:
    Bantam, 1984.

Mattson, George E. *The Way of Karate*. Vermont:
    Tuttle, 1993.

For more information please visit

www.DaveFerruolo.com

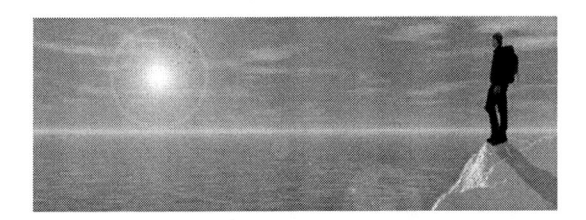

Suggested Websites:

www.ConnectingWithTheBlissOfLife.com

www.FathomDivers.com

www.TheSealTeams.com

www.DaveFerruolo.com

Elements of Life Success

David Michael Ferruolo